An Instructional Guide to the Pedal Playing of Organs

A Selection of Classic Articles on the Techniques and Practice of Pedal Playing

By

Various Authors

Copyright © 2011 Read Books Ltd.
This book is copyright and may not be
reproduced or copied in any way without
the express permission of the publisher in writing

British Library Cataloguing-in-Publication Data
A catalogue record for this book is available from
the British Library

A History of the Organ

The organ (from the Greek 'ὄργανον *organon*', meaning 'organ', 'instrument' or 'tool') is a keyboard instrument of one or more divisions, each played with its own keyboard, played either with the hands or the feet. The organ is a relatively old musical instrument in the Western musical tradition, dating from the time of Ctesibius of Alexandria who is also credited with inventing the 'hyrdraulis'. The organ gradually assumed a prominent place in the liturgy of the Catholic Church, and has subsequently re-emerged as a secular and recital instrument.

There are many different types of organs; pipe organs, reed organs, chord organs, electronic organs and steam organs. Pipe Organs, using wind moving through pipes to produce sounds are the most common however. Since the sixteenth century, pipe organs have used various materials of pipes, which can vary widely in timbre and volume – the historical successor of the panpipe. The instruments themselves can also vary greatly in size, ranging from a cubic yard to a height reaching five floors with over 10,000 pipes; usually built in churches, synagogues, concert halls, and very occasionally – homes. The pipe organ is one of the grandest musical instruments, both in its size and scope, and has existed in its current form since the fourteenth century. Other designs, such as the hydraulic organ were already used in antiquity though. Along with the clock, it was considered one of the most complex human-made mechanical creations before the Industrial Revolution.

Wolfgang Amadeus Mozart called the organ the 'King of Instruments', and perhaps its most distinctive feature is the ability to range from the slightest sound to the most powerful. For instance, the Wanamaker organ, located in Philadelphia, USA, has sonic resources comparable with three simultaneous symphony orchestras. Such instruments were first utilised (largely in church settings) in the seventh century – traditionally attributed to Pope Vitalian. Due to its simultaneous ability to provide a musical foundation below the vocal register, support in the vocal register and increased brightness above the vocal register, the organ was ideally suited to accompany human voices, whether a congregation, a choir or a cantor or soloist. Organ production continued into the medieval period too, when the first portable instruments were created, alongside a 'positive organ' – a somewhat larger, though still portable instrument. In the sixteenth century, ineffective resonance pipes were removed and the 'regal', an ancestor of the modern 'squeezebox' was invented.

Alongside the pipe variant, 'reed organs' – otherwise known as the harmonium were the other main type of organ before the development of electronic instruments. These instruments generated sounds using reeds similar to those of a piano accordion, and were generally smaller, cheaper and more portable than the corresponding pipe instrument. Their volume and tonal range was greatly limited however, and they were limited to one or two manuals; pedal-boards being extremely rare. 'Chord organs' are the other main variant, and they were invented by Laurens Hammond in 1950. This type of organ provided chord buttons for the left hand, similar to an accordion – and could also be used in 'reed' versions too. However, since the 1930s, pipeless electric instruments have also grown in popularity. Far smaller and cheaper to buy than a corresponding pipe instrument, and in many cases portable, they have taken organ music into private homes and into dance bands and other new environments - and have almost completely replaced the reed organ.

The Hammond organ was the first successful electric organ, and it used rotating tone-wheels to produce the sound waveforms. Its system of drawbars allowed for setting volumes for specific sounds, and it could provide vibrato-like effects. Though originally produced to replace organs in the church, the Hammond organ, especially the model B-3, became popular in jazz, particularly soul jazz, and in gospel music. Since these were the roots of rock and roll, the Hammond organ became part of the rock and roll sound. It was widely used in rock and popular music during the 1960s and 1970s by bands like The Doors, Pink Floyd, Santana and Deep Purple. Its popularity resurged in pop music around 2000, in part due to the availability of **'clone-wheel organs'** that were light enough for one person to carry.

As is evident from this brief history of the Organ, it is an instrument with an exceedingly long and fascinating history. We hope the reader is encouraged to find out more, and enjoys this book.

Contents

Systematic Organ Pedal Technique and General Interpretation.
Reginald Goss Custard..*page* 1

On Organ Playing - Hints to Young Organists with Complete Method for Pedal Scales and Arpeggios. Arthur Page..........*page* 41

The Technique and Art of Organ Playing.
Clarence Dickinson...*page* 46

A System of Technical Studies in Pedal Playing for the Organ.
L. Nilson...*page* 64

Systematic Organ Pedal Technique
and General Interpretation

WORKING TO A SYSTEM

ORGAN playing of to-day, as might be expected, makes a more rigorous demand on the player's manual and pedal technique than hitherto, by reason of the responsive action and artistic advancement of the modern organ.

This little treatise has been written with a view to assisting the organ student who, after cultivating a good manual technique, perhaps by the aid of the piano in the first instance, is then confronted with the many difficulties and pitfalls in acquiring a reliable pedal action and technique. In some of the standard editions of our great organ works the pedal signs are so misleading as to hamper instead of assist the student in his studies.

In the earliest stages of pianoforte playing a system of fingering is taught which, when thoroughly mastered, becomes the foundation for accuracy and facility in manual technique.

There are, as we know, certain established rules for fingering scales and arpeggios and the correct position of the hand, the flexibility of the wrist, and so forth, and I maintain that in a somewhat modified way these rules may be applied to pedalling.

Where there is no method, but merely an attempt to do a thing anyhow, there can be no confidence in oneself. "Anyhow" is not good enough for organ pedalling, as in this, like everything else, there is a right and a wrong way of doing things. The acrobatic feats which one foot is called upon to perform are amazing, and it always seems a mystery to me how the right notes are hit upon. The other foot is completely forgotten and remains firmly planted on the swell pedal, waiting for an opportunity to make some kind of a crescendo, however futile.

In the ancient days of pump-handle swells, situated at the extreme end of the pedal-board, there was a reasonable excuse in a good many instances for this one-footed method. Organists were either content or compelled to do things with one foot which nowadays should not be tolerated for an instant. Also, there was the old-fashioned pedal-board with its straight and narrow keys and noisy and heavy action; all these drawbacks were certainly not conducive to acquiring accuracy. The advent of the radiating board with a centralised swell pedal was the first advancement in modern organ building and quickly revolutionised pedalling facilities, making it possible for both feet to have greater control over the whole pedal-board.

In the earlier primers on organ playing, the student was first taught to use only toes of both feet for consecutive long notes, leaving the heels for later consideration. This, to my mind, was entirely wrong, because from the start the need for acquiring flexibility of the ankles and also for getting accustomed to using another part of the foot on a slightly different position of the key is most essential.

It is surprising to notice how awkward a beginner is in using his heels, yet after a little practice the action becomes quite natural to him.

Practically speaking, the heels should play a greater part in pedal technique than the toes, for the reason that when a heel is in action the toe is in easy reach of a short note either up or down or even as much as an interval of a third apart, whereas when a toe is on a long note it is out of position for a short key. Alternate toe and heel work with the same foot very often prevents legato passages from being broken, and at the same time eradicates the too frequent crossing of the feet. This persistency in the use of more heel action brings me considerably nearer to my subject—*systematic* pedalling. The question may be asked: can there be any useful system? Do you not just put down the note with the foot which is nearest and most convenient and trust to luck with the next one? All this, I fear, is only too true. I have watched organists with a brilliant manual technique do the most appalling things on the pedal board, with no thought of playing a particular passage twice in the same way. The uncertainty of how best to pedal a particular passage is considerably diminished if there is some method to fall back upon, and by applying this method one can be sure of executing it in the same way every time.

In the subsequent chapters I will endeavour to explain as simply as possible a system which for many years has proved successful with my pupils who, in even the dullest cases, have in a short time been able to acquire confidence and accuracy in their pedal technique. The chapter on position will be wholly devoted to explaining the scheme, and all the examples will be quoted from the works of J. S. Bach as being the best medium for laying the foundation of a sound and reliable technique. The chapter on action will deal with the important matter of foot control, knee action, suppleness of the ankles, etc., after which a few examples will be quoted from the standard works showing how the system works in passages of varying difficulty. These examples may prove useful to the student for reference purposes. The last chapter will deal in a general way with three vital matters — phrasing, accentuation and registration, under the heading of "Interpretation." Although this chapter is not strictly in accordance with the main title of the treatise, it has a direct bearing upon the subject in so far as interpretation is not wholly confined to those things which are done with the hands alone but rather with hands and feet.

POSITION

BEFORE deciding which is the correct position for the feet on the pedal board the student is advised to adopt the simple method of putting both feet together and allowing them to rest above two central long keys on the board, say D and E, with the toes almost touching the short keys in front. He will then observe that considerable overlapping takes place and the toes get in the way of one another, with the result that the key would have to be struck more on the side than in the centre. If one foot is moved back until it is in a line with the instep of the other the position is improved. Now cross over with the foremost foot and notice the result: the heel of this foot is fouling the toe of the other. This, to say the least of it, is a clumsy and inelegant procedure and could not possibly be a safe method of performing a scale of long notes only. Let us try another position by putting a heel on one note and a toe on the adjacent long key. It will be seen by this position, with one foot slightly in advance of the other, that there is no interference between the two. Crossing is now a comparatively easy

It really means the manipulation of a middle note, either a long or short key, the notes on each side being played with the same foot.

The next note E in the scale must be right toe to enable the left to cross to F♯

The obvious procedure will then be—G left heel and A♯ and B right toe and heel, thus completing the minor scale.

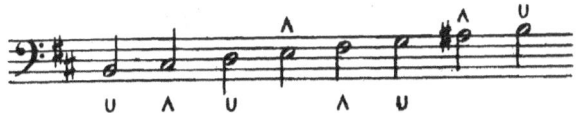

Before leaving the subject of scales, it will be as well to deal with one mostly consisting of short keys. D♭, for instance, is a typical example because of the proximity of three short keys. The first two notes must be allotted to the left foot, otherwise if the right is allowed to play E♭ we come into difficulties at once as the left must go behind, which would destroy our position and also compel the right to take all the remaining notes of the scale. F, then, is taken by the right toe, two short keys with the left and the remainder with the right, making a long note the pivot between two short ones.

It will be seen at (*a*) that two toes occur in the middle of the scale (F and G♭), but as one of the notes is a short key and with the right well back on the F there is ample room to cross over. Up till now all the examples have been illustrated in the most comfortable part of the pedal board. Passages lying at the extremes of the board, either diatonic or chromatic, are, as a general rule, best managed with one foot, unless, of course, the particular passage is continuous in one position, when it will be necessary for one foot to help the other with the body slightly turned to preserve one's balance and ensure freedom of ankle work.

The bottom octave of the pedal board is used far more frequently than the top, and the awkward position of the left foot makes it difficult to acquire smooth playing. There is a temptation to hop from note to note with the toe; this is to be deprecated as it destroys evenness of tone and is liable to lead the student into bad habits. The natural radiation of the foot will decide the use of toe and heel. On two consecutive long notes, the heel being turned inwards will command the upper note. In a similar manner with three consecutive long keys the heel will command the middle note.

The same applies to the upper register.

The use of two long keys and then a short one is not recommended with one foot as the toe is now out of position for the short key, and an inelegant slide with the heel would be necessary. It is well to remember that there is another foot to come to the rescue rather than to take the chance of smudgy pedalling and broken phrases too often caused by relying on one foot to do the work of two. In extended chromatic passages the right toe should be used on long keys only—well back so as to allow the left to operate on alternative long and short keys, thus preserving the position of left in front and right behind. This, of course, does not apply to the extremes of the board, when the last three notes at least may be taken with one foot.

Having established our position with scale formation, the subject of broken chords and arpeggio passages can now be dealt with. As will be seen later, although strict adherence to alternate toe and heel action will not be so rigidly enforced the relative feet positions will remain the same. It stands to reason that where the notes are not adjacent to one another there will be less crossing of feet; but when a passage leaps an octave with one intermediate note, crossing is necessary to preserve the phrasing and smoothness of the part. The following is an illustration taken from the G minor Fugue :—

With a little practice this is quite easy, remembering to keep the right well back. Swing the body slightly as the left heel comes up to the D and the toe is then in position for the F♯. An alternative footing is unsafe at speed.

The phrasing is bound to be broken in this case. Occasionally passages are to be met with in which we say that the notes do not lie conveniently under the fingers or feet and consequently no systematic treatment is possible. This applies to all other instruments, and is particularly noticeable if the composer has not an intimate knowledge of the instrument for which he is writing. One can cite many arrangements of piano or orchestral works that are quite unsuitable for the organ, both in the manual and pedal parts, and all that can be said of these arrangements is that they do not " come off," and it would be sheer waste of time to attempt to unravel their difficulties and, in some cases, impossibilities. Passages where alternative notes for the left foot are scale-wise can be played with toe and heel :—

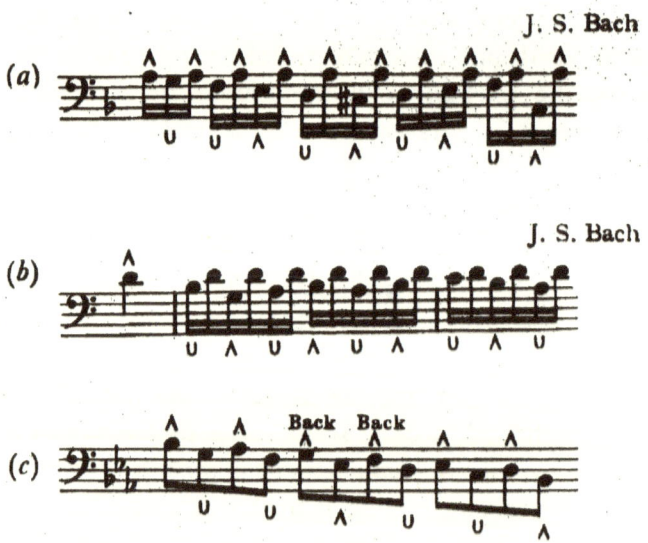

In example (c) note the action of the right foot which, after being in front for the short key A♭, takes its place behind again for G in order to preserve the position.

It will also be observed that note C must be taken with the heel so as to avoid two toes on consecutive long notes. If the passage terminated on the second G, or proceeded upwards, this note would be more conveniently placed for the right heel.

It will be seen now that the right foot is foremost in this phrase for the obvious reason that the upper notes are nearly all short keys. If the passage were in G major, the position would be reversed : *Right behind, left in front.*

The question may be asked : Why not heels on upper notes ? There is no reason why this should not be so, but as it would not facilitate matters at all, is it worth while altering the position of the feet ? These examples have been given to impress upon the student the fact that although a particular passage can be pedalled in some other way quite comfortably it is better to adhere to a system whereby confusion is eliminated and the risk of playing it in a different position each time greatly diminished.

Some of the most difficult passages to manage are the arpeggios. They cover a wide range of the pedal board, and the distribution of the feet is often a problem to solve. As a matter of fact, arpeggios of more than one octave are seldom to be found in organ music, as the extended forms are ineffective and extremely difficult to play connectedly ; but for the sake of argument and for systematic purposes a few examples of two octaves will be given. The main point, to remember is to do as little crossing as possible, and then only at the interval of a third (major or minor), in the centre of the board.

Notes at the extremes must be managed with one foot with the exception of D♭ and E♭ upwards, in which case the second notes F and G respectively must be played with the right foot. In each case if the first three notes are played with the left the right becomes placed in an awkward position on the fourth note, and the following long note would either mean the left coming behind or taking all the remaining notes with the right foot, thus :—

Whichever way this is played it is clumsy and inelegant and does not comply with the system.

The correct pedalling will be :—

The arpeggio of E♭ should be pedalled in the same way. The only two arpeggios consisting of nothing but short keys, being E♭ minor and F♯ major, will need a little consideration. It stands to reason that no actual crossing of the feet takes place, and it is a matter of one foot being drawn smartly back to enable the other to operate on the higher or lower note as the case may be. The best position for the change is at the interval of the perfect fourth, the feet having more chance of disentangling themselves on the wide interval;

fortunately, extended passages on short keys are few and far between. E♭ minor would be pedalled thus :—

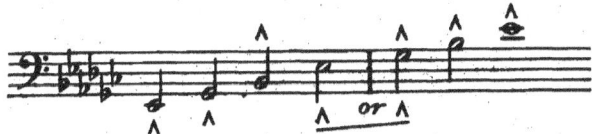

F♯ major in the same way.

Arpeggios in the remaining keys are more or less pedalled to a pattern, the first three notes at the extremes working on a pivot note. As in the case of chromatic passages, the right foot should be used as much as possible on the long keys, but if it is brought forward for a short one it must immediately take up the position behind again.

The examples in C and E major will suffice as patterns :—

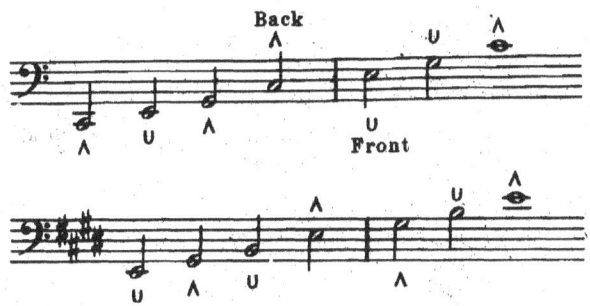

Diminished chords can be pedalled much in the same way as common chords. They are easier to negotiate by reason of the fact that the long and short keys are more evenly divided. The compass seldom exceeds the octave in real organ music; in which case more often than not crossing is unnecessary. For instance, the following example is quite easy and comfortable :—

Any extension of the above would necessitate crossing, and it will be as well to remind the student again that, as in the chromatic scale, the right foot will only operate on long keys (back) :—

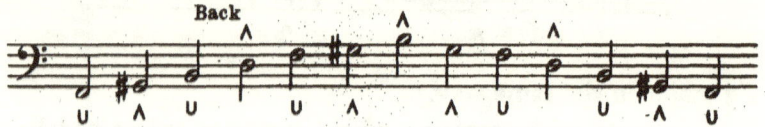

It is needless to give other examples as the other keys will be modelled on the same lines. We repeat what was said at the beginning : that the extended form of both common and diminished chords is seldom to be met with in organ music, and that these examples have only been given to verify the system, yet in a modified form the student will be able to frame his own ideas as to their treatment.

Pedal passages of a sequential nature, particularly when the figure is diatonic, specially lend themselves to systematic treatment and make an interesting study. We cannot do better than refer to some of the famous fugue subjects of Bach as concrete examples : in particular the Toccata in F, the D major and minor Fugues and the great G minor. In all these works there are long stretches of sequential passages diatonically constructed which can be patterned, as it were, with a uniform system of pedalling. This does not mean to say that every figure can be footed in the same manner, as the position of the long and short keys in the pattern must necessarily decide the position of the feet. Take, for example, the D major fugue subject. According to the system no other alternative is possible for the first entry than the following :—

While the right is stationary on B the left is negotiating a major third with scarcely any movement whatever—in fact, the third could be played simultaneously with ease and comfort. This passage is more often than not played with two notes to one foot. Try it and see the difference.

The second entry in the tonic key is similar, but in the B minor and F♯ entries we have to resort to two notes with one foot unless the left is put behind on the long key, which is less satisfactory and unsafe. The next phrase in the subject gives a definite example of pattern playing, as it is sequential. Here is the pattern :—

The entire sequence can be pedalled on this model.

Before we leave the D major Fugue an excellent example will be found in the solo passage at the end. The passage is sequential for two octaves comprising the whole range of the pedal board, starting thus :—

The pattern is the same for the next three sequences :—

After which the pattern is slightly altered by commencing with the left heel :—

It will be observed that no crossing of feet occurs in the whole passage.

The next and last example is the pedal solo in Bach's Toccata in F. The rising sequence in the first four bars makes it possible to pedal each bar in the same manner, the lowest note in each group being played with the toe of the left—not heel :—

As the left foot notes skip an interval of a fourth and fifth there is no object in using all heels—it is not only unsafe but inelegant. The passage is similar to the one in the D minor fugues, where alternate notes are taken with toe and heel, except in the case of two adjacent long keys where the heel of the left must, of course, be used.

The next six bars consist of a falling sequence, and it will be noted that the lower notes are repeated in scale form. All these will be taken with heel of the left foot as there is no object in changing the position on reiterated notes. The three highest notes in the eleventh and thirteenth bars may be played with the right foot if preferred. The succeeding pedal solo in the dominant key will be pedalled in the same manner. The student will be able to find numerous examples in other standard organ works where sequential passages can be pedalled to a pattern, and considerable interest should be derived from working out the system for himself as set out in this chapter.

ACTION

IN the last chapter we dealt entirely with the position of the feet on the pedal-board based upon a systematic scheme. There is a great deal that can be said with regard to foot-control: for instance, the correct action of toe and heel, flexibility of ankle and freedom of the knees, etc.

To begin with, a word about footwear will not be out of place here. The student need not be fastidious about this, but there is no doubt that shoes are more convenient than boots, because the ankles are afforded freedom, whereas a heavy boot is inflexible and cumbersome on the pedal. Shoes with fairly stout soles with the toes not too pointed are best, and some people prefer to keep a pair of shoes for organ playing only. The inconvenience of carrying special footwear about seems unnecessary, however, and ordinary walking shoes are all that are needed; but, of course, rubber heels are fatal.

It is a common fault of the beginner to use the flat of the foot on a key, with the result that two notes are liable to be sounded together. This is either due to the stool being too low or the inability to give sufficient action to the ankles. The seat should be just high enough to enable the player to rest his feet lightly on the face of the keys. Having made the correct adjustment (most stools now are adjustable), be careful to raise the heel for toe playing and the toe for heeling. The foot should never be allowed to strike the key edgeways, as bad habits very quickly develop, and when any speed is required smudgy playing will be the result. Another common fault is for the player to shuffle from one long key to another by means of toe and heel action on the same note, which really means that he intends playing two consecutive long keys with the toe by using the heel as a pivot. This is quite unnecessary, as loss of time must occur, to say nothing about bad pedalling.

The note which is being operated should have the toe or heel, as the case may be, in position for the next long key. Pedalling with facility and ease will depend a great deal on the early tuition in organ playing. There are many dodges which are supposed to assist the player in finding his way about the pedal board. One in particular: when the leap of a wide interval is taken with either foot the gap between the two sets of short keys is frequently used as a means of intimating the position of the note to be played. For instance, if the leap of a fifth, say, from D to lower G, is required, F♯ is automatically felt for before G can be located. Such a practice as this is contrary to all laws of organ pedalling, and it is impossible to see how any progress can be made, or speed attained, by what might be called a lack of confidence on the part of the student. How then does one manage to leap accurately without looking down at the feet? It is certainly not by guesswork, neither is it by making a particular spot on the pedal-board a "refuge in time of need."

Instinctively distance by intervals is the surest method. The leap of anything greater than an octave is seldom executed with the same foot, and, if this is the case, one might ask the question, *What is the other foot doing?* Intervals of a 2nd or 3rd are easy enough because the keys are adjacent enough to allow of a legato action with toe and heel, or *vice versa*. Skips of a 4th or 5th require more judgment, there being a definite action of the foot for these intervals. It was stated in the last chapter that the natural radiation of the foot will decide the position of toe and heel on two consecutive long notes. We will take, for example, a skip from bottom C to its 5th, played with toe and heel alternatively. As the foot moves upwards a distinct inward curve will be apparent, and an outward one for the opposite direction. This is due to the radiation of the foot and the forward position of the heel when it comes to rest on the upper note. If both notes are taken with the toe of the same foot proceeding in almost a straight line, the interval is liable to be misjudged. Taking into account the distance the foot has to travel for the interval of an octave, this method would not apply, therefore it is better to use toes for both notes. These skips with one foot are generally confined to the lower part of the pedal-board when the other foot cannot be spared from the swell pedal and also when the bass notes are intermittent.

Another important action is that of playing two or even three consecutive short keys with the same foot. Shuffling or wriggling from one to another is a bad practice, there being a danger of both notes sounding simultaneously. The action should be definite by slightly raising the foot before proceeding to the next note, the movement being smart enough to avoid breaking the legato.

Never slide off a short key on to the next long one with the toe, there is always a heel ready. Changing feet on the same note requires neatness of action. If the change is being made upwards, slide the right toe back and put the left heel in front. In the opposite direction put the right toe behind the left heel. It is impossible to try to place two toes on the same key, as the heel of the foremost foot will foul the other foot. Care should be taken to see that the key is not released during the change. If the note is a repeated one, as in the following example by J. S. Bach, the position of the feet will be the same, but the release of the toe must be prompt.

Talking about the prompt release of keys brings us to the subject of staccato action. To be effective, very much depends upon the promptness of speech of the 16 ft. pipes. It is not an uncommon occurrence to come across fine organs with perfect manual actions, beautiful voicing, instantaneous stop control, etc., but leaving much to be desired in the pedal department, which fails entirely to respond to any kind of staccato action. However, as this is not a treatise on organ construction we must assume that the instrument will do what is required of it.

The pedal staccato should be quite as definite as the manual staccato, but difficulty arises in keeping the action consistent throughout the passage. One of the most difficult tasks in teaching the organ is that of imparting to the student the necessity of acquiring a separate action with another part of the body, the feet invariably wanting to do what the hands are doing. For pedal staccato the toes can be used more frequently, especially in the lower part of the board when a passage is permissible with one foot only. In the case of scale formation the position and footing must be the same as for legato playing, otherwise confusion and bad pedalling will be the result. The release of the key is the most important factor. Semi-staccato requires a firm pressure with a quick release, but a real staccato, giving the idea of a *pizz*. *Double Bass* effect, is executed by a sharp tap with the toe, just sufficient to depress the key. No knee movement is necessary; the ankle will do all that is required.

The following examples will help to explain the various types of staccato :—

The action in this example must be semi-detached throughout, taking care that evenness of tone is regular.

The combined legato and staccato action here is very important, as it is a repetition of the left hand in the opening bars. As the passage is in scale form, alternative use of toe and heel will be necessary and definite phrasing is required to make it effective.

The staccato in this movement should be very short, the toe just tapping the key in order to give the *pizz.* effect. Notice that toes only are used.

In considering knee and body action a great deal may be said for feeling at ease at the keyboard. A stool which is too high or too low, a badly scaled pedal-board or a cramped console for lack of space are serious drawbacks from the player's point of view. The stool should be dead straight with the keyboards, and in such a position that it will not interfere with the balance of the body when playing on the upper manual. Some organists appear to make organ playing hard labour, the body swaying from side to side and their pedal action appearing as if a treadmill were being operated. There is really no necessity for these contortions of the body, as the action of the modern organ has made everything so easy and comfortable for the player. A steady upright position as far as possible should be aimed at, the body turning naturally with the radiation of the feet as they reach towards the extremes of the pedal-board. In a long pedal solo the question is often asked, Where should the hands be ? The body undoubtedly requires some kind of support, otherwise the balance is easily upset, and the best method is to place the palms of the hands on the stool with the fingers overlapping the edge. This position will tend to steady the body and give the necessary freedom to the feet—folded arms are a mistake.

Knee action is just as important as ankle action. In all pedal passages where the feet are close together the knees should be in a similar position. Any sprawling attitude will upset the proper action of the feet, and the key will be struck on the side, thereby causing inaccuracy and loss of speed. Rapidity is chiefly acquired through freedom at the knee joint, and any stiffness at this point will tire the player in any long spell of pedal work.

The student is recommended to spend some time in making himself efficient in these various actions by practising scales and arpeggios together with some of the well-known pedal passages to be found in the works of Bach. It will repay him over and over again.

Before concluding this chapter, one item of importance must not be overlooked—the action of the foot on the swell pedal.

Assuming that the balanced type of pedal is in use and the organ a moderately sized three-manual with an enclosed choir organ, the swell pedal, which is the more frequently used, should be on the right of the choir pedal for obvious reasons.

Balanced swell pedals vary, not only in position but also in weight. This is more a matter of taste, although a very light pedal does not give the best results. Swell shutters are very sensitive (or should be), and unless a proper balance is attained great difficulty will be experienced in effecting a gradual increase and decrease of tone. The foot should be firmly planted on the pedal with the weight evenly distributed —for opening, press with the toe, keeping the heel well down on the lever; any attempt to operate the pedal with the toe only will make it impossible to obtain a gradual crescendo. For closing, press with the heel without raising the toe. In the case of a sudden decrescendo it is always permissible to do so with the toe on the edge of the pedal. Expression on the organ is not entirely dependent upon the swell shutters as some people are led to believe; neither is the organ an expressionless instrument as we are told by some musicians who are not and never were organists. Phrasing, for instance, is one of the greatest assets for expressing the music in an intellectual manner. So many organists forget the fact and are content to rely upon the swell pedal for expressing their emotions. Organ accent is too often unregarded, and a piece becomes lifeless and dull. However, these other means of expression on the organ will be dealt with in the chapter on interpretation. The swell pedal is a dangerous weapon for the student who is starting for the first time to put expression into his pieces. The common fault is to put the right foot on the pedal and keep it there! So much inaccuracy in pedalling is caused by this practice. Why will organ composers and arrangers write expression marks where it is impossible to regard them? In a good many instances neither hands nor feet are available for any increase of tone, and the most we can do is to manipulate a thumb piston which does the wrong thing at the wrong moment. Although the modern organ provides so many accessories and gadgets for controlling the instrument, the fact remains that it is still a difficult matter to obtain a really artistic crescendo without the tone being doled out in " chunks."

Let the student therefore first acquire a sound pedal technique before attempting to apply his activity to organ playing.

APPLICATION

THERE are many pedal passages in the standard works of organ composers, and particularly among the modern organ compositions, which present not only to the students, but to players of experience, considerable difficulties, and unless some system is adhered to the particular pedal passage is in danger of being inaccurately played every time. It must be stated that no system is entirely infallable, but in the following examples it will be found that only one or two alternative examples do not conform to the system which the writer has endeavoured to explain in the preceding chapters. The rule for left heel in front and right toe behind must be rigidly enforced unless otherwise stated. The first example, quoted for phrasing in the last chapter, would appear on paper to be quite easy, because it has no sharps or flats, but many keyboard executants will declare that the scale of C major is as difficult as any to play neatly. This is also the case on the pedal-board :—

The two upper notes are taken with the right foot in order that the lowest note D of the scale may be played with the left.

Downward scales from the middle of the pedal-board :—

It will be noticed that when a long and short note occur consecutively both may be taken with the same foot. The low A in the second scale is given to the right to avoid a clumsy action with the left on the last two notes. An alternative footing with the right toe on the second minim will alter the pedalling slightly, but either example is correct.

The augmented interval two bars later need not entail any alteration in the pedal marks, but the C natural will be a little more awkward to manage.

The next example of downward scales will present little difficulty if the first scale is taken more or less as a pattern:—

Prelude and Fugue in D minor. Bach (Dorian)

The first three notes in bar 3 should be taken with the right foot to avoid the feet clashing on the semitone, E♭ to D.

A similar passage in ascending scales is interesting :—

Fugue in E minor. (Wedge) Bach

In the 2nd scale the short notes must be taken with the left foot, otherwise the left will have to go behind on the E, thus destroying the position of the feet.

The next example is difficult :—

Finale 1st Sonata. Guilmaut

The rising thirds interspersed with tone and semitone and the right hand manual part in contrary motion with the pedals, is always liable to give trouble unless a definite footing is decided upon. The first five notes may be a pattern for the next four, which means that the feet cross once in each case. The semitone E and F must be taken with the left foot, otherwise it will mean crossing again on the last two upper notes, which would not be advisable here on account of speed. If in the first three lowest notes the F had been sharp all three could have been taken with one foot, thus avoiding the right getting down to G; but to commence in this fashion would be clumsy and unsafe at speed.

A similar passage in a modern work in the reverse position may be quoted :—

Finale 1st Sym.   Vierne

As both hands are stationary all attention can be given to the pedal passage. It will be seen that the feet do not cross until the lower D in order that the body may move slightly with the downward motion of the passage. The repeated F♯ and E are best taken with the left. We give an alternative footing for this passage, which may, perhaps, appeal to some players.

The repeated F♯ and E are taken with separate feet, which entails more crossing afterwards. However, both pedallings conform to the system and with a little practice become comparatively easy. Before leaving the subject of scales, one typical example of a chromatic scale involving the entire range of the pedal-board may be useful:—

This passage is simple if the student will remember to use the right foot on long keys and the left on the short ones as stated in an earlier chapter. In order to do this the first three notes must be taken with the left foot.

Some examples will now be given of passages which, if not always difficult in themselves, become more involved by the technicality of the manual parts. Space will not admit of the manual parts being given, but in each case the particular passage can easily be found in the works:—

These passages immediately following one another, although similar in construction, need entirely different pedalling:—At (*a*) in the third group of semiquavers the heel of the left passes over on the D, and at (*b*) at the same point the toe of the left must pass over to the E♭. Note the alternative heel and toe in the following arpeggio passage at (*b*). The manual parts in both cases will need careful phrasing and legato movement.

Fugue in G minor. Dupré

This passage occurs at the end of the work, and is awkward because of the contrary motion on the manual. The three sections of four notes each mark the entry of the hands in succession, thereby defining the phrasing. Two heels occur on the fourth and fifth notes respectively, otherwise the whole of section 2 must be taken with the right foot, which would be unsafe at speed. The change of feet on the B♭ at the end of section 2 and the beginning of section 3 is imperative.

Two examples from Bach's Trio Sonatas contain features which have not yet been met with :—

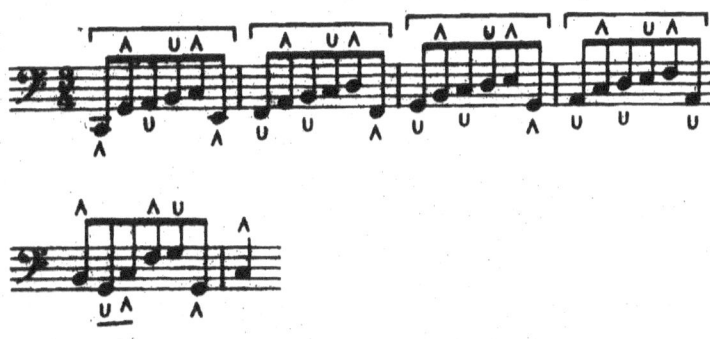

Sonata No. 5. 1st movement. Bach

The whole passage being sequential on long keys, each sequence can be pedalled alike, taking the first as a pattern.

The right hand manual part is again in contrary motion which adds somewhat to its difficulties :—

Sonata No. 2. 1st movement. Bach

In each case the upper notes of the groups must, of course, be played with the right foot, and in order to obtain a neat action the heel must slide back slightly on the G so as to avoid the toe fouling the F♯. Many examples might be quoted where this action is most useful; it is quite clear that no other pedalling is possible for this passage.

Another passage of considerable difficulty will be found in the first movement of Widor's Sixth Symphony where, owing to the fact that it is confined to the bottom octave of the pedal-board, together with its speed, the left foot has to do most of the work whichever way it is pedalled.

6th Symphony. Widor

The left foot could be slightly relieved by taking the E♭ in the first bar with the right. The awkward skip of an augmented fourth from the D to G♯ in the second bar cannot be avoided unless the G♯ is taken with the right and the left passed behind on the A and again on the C. This, however, is contrary to the system and would scarcely improve matters. Thus :—

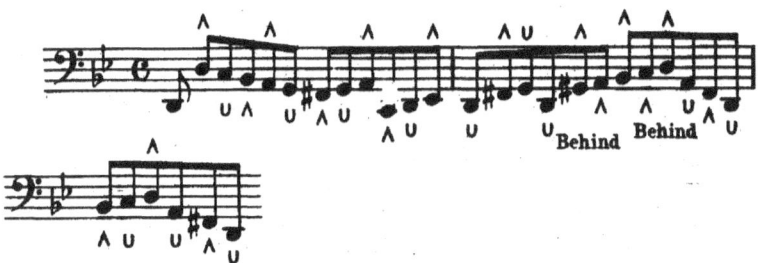

Arpeggios mostly on short keys must be conveniently distributed between both feet, as it is obvious that no crossing can take place.

Dithyramb.   Basil Harwood

The last illustration to be given is a pedal cadenza comprised of semi-tones.

It will be better to use alternate feet here rather than to take two notes with one foot. The knee action will help to execute the passage clearly and greatly encourage speed.

The trills in each case will be taken with left heel and right toe.

In the foregoing examples of varied types an attempt has been made to convince the student that the system will work itself out in every case, however complicated the passage may seem at first sight. Badly laid-out pedal passages will conform to no system just as in the same way a composer with little or no knowledge of strings, wood-wind or brass is apt to score passages for the instruments which are either out of the compass or are extremely difficult to execute. The student will no doubt during his organ studies come across passages similar to those already illustrated, and if he will take the trouble to work out the pedalling on the same lines the writer believes that his task of overcoming difficulties will be considerably lessened.

INTERPRETATION

However perfect an organist's pedal technique may be, it does not necessarily follow that his studies are at an end with regard to organ playing. The act of phrasing, both on the manual and pedals, the control of the expressive departments by means of the swell pedal, together with a judicious management of the stops, either by hand or mechanical means, all these things are vitally important to the student who is desirous of becoming a first-rate organist.

An organist's career nearly always commences by accompanying a church service, a simple one perhaps, requiring little skill but an immense amount of good taste and restraint. An artist is more readily detected by his or her accompaniment of the psalms and hymns rather than by a showy voluntary. As a general rule, more time and thought could easily be spent on these essential portions of the church service. The writer contends that one of the best mediums for acquiring a sound pedal technique is by playing a hymn tune in four-part harmony with the pedal-board assigned to its proper pitch and not, as is so often the case, with the left foot jumping about in a staccato manner over the bottom octave of the pedal-board. A little thought will convince the student that such a practice is not only inartistic but ineffective. The ponderous tones of the 16 ft. pipes destroy the clarity of the harmony, and if used for verse after verse it becomes monotonous and aggravating to the choir and congregation. The habit of keeping the right foot continually on the swell pedal and unconsciously working the lever up and down is a bad one, and the sooner it is overcome the better. This does not mean to say that bottom octave pedalling should never be resorted to; sparingly used the effect is called for, thereby showing the resourcefulness of the player. What a relief it is to hear a verse or two of a hymn played in pure four-part harmony without pedals! A fact so often overlooked is that the choir are present to lead the singing, not the organ to lead the choir. Sudden bursts of sounds from the organ with handfuls of chords are always ineffective, especially if manual doubles are being used at the same time. The doubled major third, as we know, is harsh and should be rigidly avoided in four-part harmony.

Reference was made in the preceding chapter with regard to other means of expression than by the medium of the swell pedal, *i.e.*, phrasing and accentuation. Without these attributes no music can be intelligible. The organ, unlike any other keyed instrument, is not expressive at the key, so we are entirely dependent upon mechanical means of expression in this respect. The swell pedal is for producing varied degrees of tone and the stops for the individual quality of tone and power, each of which is mechanically controlled. The act of phrasing, the sense of rhythm and accentuation, do not, of course, come under the category of mechanical control but are solely dependent upon the musicianship of the organist and should be applied to organ playing to an extent which will make up for, and to a certain extent take the place of, the other means of expression, which are only mechanically obtained. No instrument is more sensitive to legato playing than the organ by reason of the fact that the action is on the top of the key, and unless a definite release is effected the endings of phrases cannot be completed. Therefore phrasing on the organ must be slightly more exaggerated than on the piano. Another point to remember is that unless the building is exceptionally "dead" the resonance prolongs the sound beyond the phrases and the music becomes incoherent. The observance of phrase marks for the pedals (when indicated !) is not always thought of by the student as important. This is a great mistake, because the pedal part does not merely supply the bass notes to a chord but, as in all music, it must necessarily form part of the music structure as a whole, and frequently in a melodic capacity. Even in the simple four-part harmony of hymns and psalms the pedal part should be in keeping with the manuals. Nothing is more irritating than to hear a hymn being played legato on the manual and staccato on the bass and void of all phrase observances at the end of the lines.

Good phrasing and accentuation are the hall-marks of a true artist, and an organ, however large and resourceful, cannot fail to reveal its mechanical defects and other shortcomings in the hands of a player who is lacking in what might be termed the most vital attribute of the organ's means of expression. A great many of the standard works of the earlier organ composers are sadly in need of re-editing, if only on account of the phrasing marks. The following example from Rheinberger's Twelfth Sonata will show how hopelessly misleading the signs are :—

According to these groupings, it would be an impossibility to emphasise the accent on the second beat of the bar, thus losing the sense of syncopation entirely. If phrased in this manner :—

we at once preserve that rhythmical accent which surely was the composer's intention.

Dr. Harvey Grace's new edition of the Rheinberger Sonatas should be a valuable help to the student. Not only has the phrasing been given careful consideration, but also some helpful suggestions for manual changes and stop registration have been added.

The phrasing of a fugue subject should be clearly defined at its first entry, and every part treated in the same manner. When the pedals enter, the phrasing is sometimes almost a nonentity, whereas this part is in need of just as much careful phrasing as the others, because the heavy 16 ft.

tones are apt to destroy the rhythm and settle the whole fugue down to a dead level. Although there is more than one way of phrasing certain fugue subjects, the following examples are generally accepted as being the most authentic :—

Great G minor

A major

A minor

D minor (Dorian)

St. Anne

In the Bach Trio Sonatas unending opportunities will be found for developing the art of phrasing, both on the manuals and pedals. Many instances occur where 8 ft. tone only on the pedals is called for ; every part there is in the same pitch and will require that amount of individuality which tends to preserve the interest of the work as a whole.

ACCENTUATION. Although the organ is expressionless at the key, accentuation is not impossible. It *must* be possible, otherwise the music will be void of all rhythmical sense. We certainly have not that facility for producing accent as on the piano, for instance, where a particular melody note or inner part can be reinforced, but we have considerable command over the organ by means of the swell pedal, either in ensemble or solo work. The crescendo pedal (or its more ancient title, sforzando pedal) is not the slightest use as a means of accentuation for the simple reason that reinforcement is obtained by adding at the moment other tone colours which will not blend with the rest of the phrase. A sforzando $<sf>$ is not quite equivalent to an accent $>$. This is a point which is sometimes overlooked. The swell pedal is capable of producing an effective accent by opening the box a little below half-way and shutting it smartly while the note or chord is being played. If the shutters operate rapidly, as they should, accent is possible either in chord or solo work. The only other means is by isolation, or, in other words, by breaking up the tone in front of the accent. This, of course, is achieved by definitely lifting the hands from the keys at the exact moment of accentuation. A group of FF chords with emphasis on each is a good example, for if these chords are not struck with technical precision no accent can possibly be effected.

RHYTHM, or the sub-division of accent, is as valuable an asset to the organist as phrasing and accentuation. Reference has already been made to the fact that the organ is more susceptible to legato playing than any other keyed instrument. This being so, it is an easy matter, if we are not careful, to smooth out one's playing, as it were, until the rhythm is scarcely defined at all. The great toccatas and fugues by Bach are the finest examples of rhythmical music.

The making or marring of a work depends upon the

player's sense of rhythm. It is a very common fault to hear a fugue subject with its pace set too fast to be consistent throughout, for when the pedals enter the speed has to be reduced in order to comply with the performer's limited capabilities in pedal technique. On the other hand, nothing is more wearisome than to listen to a toccata or fugue played under speed, as the music immediately becomes lifeless and unrhythmical.

On the whole, the tendency is to play too fast on the organ. Bach especially is played at a greater speed in this country than in Germany or France. The modern action is perhaps partly responsible for this, as the absence of key resistance undoubtedly gets the better of the player's technical powers, whereby rhythm and accent run riot for want of rigidity and control.

REGISTRATION. However useful and necessary stop-controls may be in the modern organ, the fact must not be overlooked that hand registration is still one of the most essential factors in organ playing. Stereotyped effects can never take the place of individual tone-colour, there being so many occasions where the desired effect cannot be obtained from mechanical controls. The diapasons, as we know, are the foundation of organ tone, but their beauty and pureness are so often hidden by contrasting colours. A single diapason in chorales, fugue subjects and even in accompanying a hymn tune, is satisfying and far more effective than being used with a reed or flute tone of another pitch.

It is surprising also to note how many more individual effects can be obtained by uncoupled manuals. The great organ is too often used in conjunction with the swell, one might suppose, for the reason that unless the Great is enclosed no means of expression is available. This may be so, but it should be remembered that there are times in which it is a relief to hear those tones which are not hampered by a box round them!

The more mechanical pistons an organ possesses the greater the danger there is of the organist becoming mechanical too. It is a comparatively easy matter to register by piston, but hand registration requires thought and aptitude. A meaningless tonal scheme is just as bad as a dull and uninteresting one. This applies especially to solo work. Sometimes a melody is not allowed to pursue its course without undergoing various changes in tone-colour for no other reason than an excuse for stop-changing. When the music is of an imitative character, then, of course, the natural process is a change of tone-colour well contrasted and well-balanced. Even then in a number of cases the desired effect can be obtained on another manual which has already been prepared for, thus avoiding any break in the rhythm or phrasing. In small organs where the choice of solo stops is limited, an addition of an 8 ft. or 4 ft. flute is most effective.

It is not always possible to adhere to the composer's markings for registration, and a complete rearrangement of the tonal scheme is necessary. Recital programmes are often injudiciously chosen (especially orchestral arrangements for organs of inadequate resources), with the result that the composer's intention cannot be carried out and the interpretation becomes a ridiculous mimic of the original. Organs are not standardised with regard to the position of the stops, and it is then that registration marks become a hindrance. Arrangements therefore become rearrangements, so to speak, to suit the particular organ on which they are to be performed.

The study of fugue construction will greatly assist the student in his registration of Bach works. It is by no means an easy matter to know where to change manuals effectively, or where a particular entry on another manual can be made conspicuous. No hard and fast rule is possible on this point; it is only the musicianship of the player that can help him out of his difficulties. One thing is certain, and that is that immediately the pedals are silent this is by no means the given signal for a change of manuals. Some fugues suggest a gradual building up of the organ to a climax, others call for a quiet and unobtrusive treatment throughout, while others require a toccata-like touch with a more or less even tone throughout. For instance, one cannot imagine either the Great G minor or the Toccata in F being played on a soft organ throughout, neither can one conceive the subject of the B minor Fugue being announced on the full organ !

It may be true to say that no other organ composition needs more careful regard to registration and variety of tone-colour than the fugue. There is generally plenty of noise obscuring the clarity of the part writing by excessive use of manual doubles, tiresome misuse of swell reeds and ponderous pedals ; all these things quickly pall upon the ear and tend to make the fugue a thoroughly dull composition to listen to. If, as is the case, every fugue that Bach ever wrote can be played effectively on a two-manual instrument, how much greater are the player's facilities on a three-manual ! The third manual is able to supply the contrast to a quiet swell, especially in imitative passages or lengthy episodes, without worrying much about stop-changing. When the time comes again for building up the organ to a climax, a gradual crescendo should be aimed at, avoiding spasmodic increases of tone which, to say the least of it, are inartistic.

In conclusion, the student will observe that the whole of this chapter has been devoted to those vital points, such as phrasing, accentuation and registration, which it is to be hoped will help to assist and interest him in his organ studies from their very commencement.

PEDAL PLAYING.

29. Pedal playing is not difficult in itself, but it is a great trouble to get hands and feet to work independently, and this applies especially to the left hand, which will always want to get at the bass part if the student has previously played the pianoforte. On the whole subject of pedalling it seems to us there is a large amount of fundamental error to contend against, the toe being used too much, often to the entire exclusion of the heel, even when its use is specially desirable.

The beginner will most certainly find himself "dabbing" about the pedal-board, using the toe of the left foot only for all the pedal part, and when he is sufficiently advanced—or thinks he is—to use the swell pedal, this disease will assume a very acute form. The heels should be used as freely as the toes from the very beginning. The first exercises should be :—

not those which encourage tip-toe-ing. This "tip-toe-ing" gets the feet into a bad position. The heels are held some inches too high instead of being always as close to the keys as they can be kept. The student acquires a perpetual up and down movement from the toe to the knee, (a sort of bicycle action in miniature), which makes it difficult for him to use the heel when its turn does eventually come; which tends also to make him a noisy player and an ungainly one to look at. A good player should have scarcely any movement of the knees, the feet glide over the board easily and even gracefully, and there is nothing like an acrobatic performance.

30. The signs ∧ , ○ , indicate toe and heel. If over the notes, the right foot is intended; if under, the left.

31. We will now give a passage from one of Bach's smaller organ fugues, with two methods of playing it :—

The method just given would probably be adopted by most players, and would be considered entirely satisfactory, but that proves nothing but want of thought on their part. It is very like playing the passage with alternate hands on the manuals, and if nothing better could be found there would be no more to say.

32. In deciding how to play any passage on the pedals the first consideration should be, *what has each foot to do;* and how far can what may be called a continuous method for each be adopted. This is an important point, and one we have never seen mentioned, although it lies at the very root of the whole matter. Referring back to our example at (*a*) we find that the first and third notes have to be played with the left foot, and we see that the first of these is a short key, the other a long one. We *know* that if they were played without any intervening note, the toe and heel of the left foot would be used, and there is no reason why, in this instance, the intervening note should affect the question. To be quite clear we now give all the notes which have to be taken with the left foot, disregarding entirely for the present those for the right.

By considering the passage as we have, it almost plays itself. And no one could possibly take a wrong course, only the one given being possible, if we try to get what has been called above a continuous method for each foot. Five of the notes have been left unmarked for consideration. At *(a)*, *(b)*, and *(e)*, we give the choice to the heel because the use of the toe would bring the foot out of line. By "out of line" we mean that the foot would have to be drawn away from the short keys, and we contend that each foot should always work up and down the board on an imaginary line as far as is possible. At *(c)* and *(d)* it is perfectly obvious that the heel should be used because of the short key following.

We now turn to the share of the notes for the right foot.

The marked notes require no comment, for it is certain that the most inveterate "toe-ist" would play them as marked, if he considered them as for right foot only without any intervening notes. The first unmarked note *(a)* can be played with equal ease by either heel or toe, and the toe would be the best for getting at the D following, but this puts the "foot out of line" with the rest of the work, so again we give the preference to the heel. The remaining notes not marked do not affect the matter in any way. (We prefer playing repeated notes with toe and heel of the same foot alternately, but it is scarcely a point worth insisting on). We now give the complete passage *(b)*.

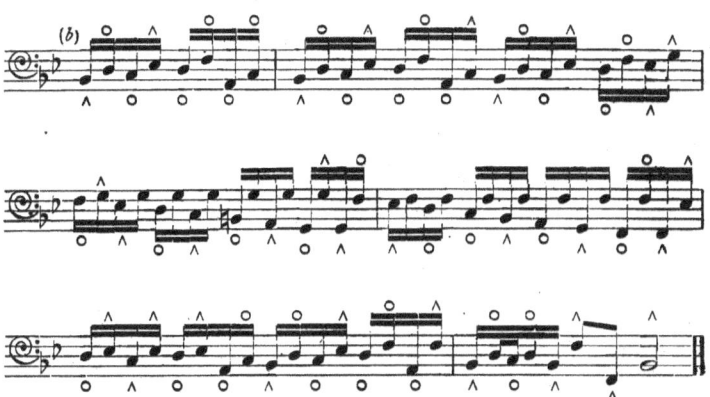

Probably the first impression of the player will be that this method is more difficult than the alternate toe plan, but it will only be his "first impression," and there can be no question which of the two is the *quieter* (a great matter in pedal-playing).

33. Scales for the pedals, as given in some "tutors," must fairly appal the beginner, and he may be pardoned if he almost despairs of ever being able to play neatly, comfortably, and quietly. Neatness of execution is, upon some of the systems advocated, impossible; comfort cannot come; and as for quietness!, the clatter is often dreadful, especially if any unusually energetic "toe-ist" is operating. We contend that any system which demands that the toe shall be almost under the organ stool one instant and then be dashed forward suddenly to get at a short key must of necessity be a bad one, and yet some writers require "alternate toes as far as possible in all scale passages," quite regardless of long or short keys. We propose to examine a few specimens.

34. For our purpose one octave will be sufficient, and, it may be added, for almost all practical purposes excepting examinations.

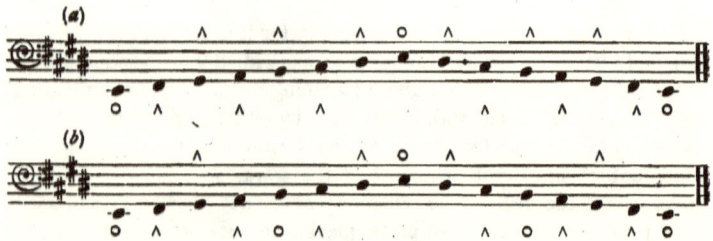

Bearing in mind our imaginary line and continuous method, we will see how far the above examples are satisfactory. In each, the left foot starts in what we are inclined to call the natural position for pedal-playing (that is, heel low and toe raised in readiness for the short keys); next, the right toe is placed on the G sharp (example *a*), and so far the plan is entirely satisfactory. But next, our instructor bids the left foot leave its position in order that the toe may be placed on A (passing under, or behind, the right foot), then the right foot is in turn drawn back to be placed on B, then the left foot goes forward again for the C sharp, and finally the right foot finishes the scale. Now, excepting the beginning and the end, this is all bad. Example (*b*) is better, but the left foot has to be pushed along the B key whilst holding it, in order to get at the C sharp, and this can be avoided. (This pushing the foot along the key is sometimes quite unavoidable). Moreover, the left foot is brought out of line by the use of the toe on A. We give another plan :—

The above method fulfils all our requirements, and is beyond all doubt neater, more comfortable, and quieter than the plan given at either (*a*) or (*b*).

It will be well, before proceeding further, to see what each foot has to do, just as we did in the example from Bach :—

The student is advised to always think out the method as shown, and even to practise the feet separately.

35. Now will follow some examples of the use of the toe where the heel would be better, (taken from "tutors" for the organ), under letter (*a*). At (*b*) in each case, is our antidote :—

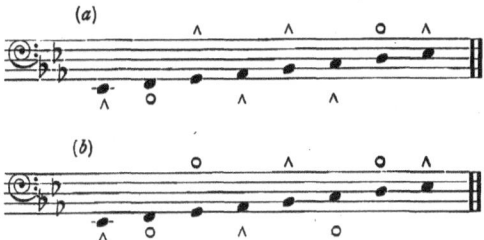

In (*a*), the left foot is quite needlessly thrown out of line. The plan at (*b*) is better. There is a little difficulty at first in using the right heel on the G with left toe to follow on A flat, to which we will allude later :—

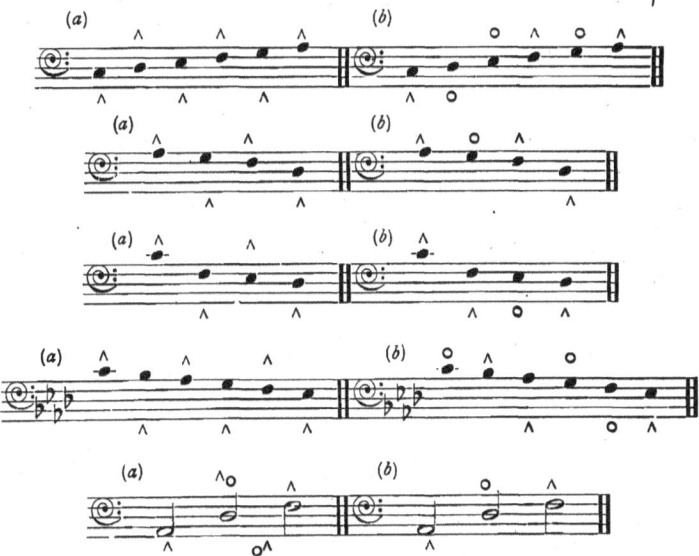

We draw special attention to the last example, where an enormous amount of trouble for absolutely no gain is recommended. Even if it were necessary to change on the D (which it is not) it would be better to put only the toe (or heel) of each foot on it instead of both. Two feet on one key are as necessary at times as are two fingers on one key, but the case we give is an absurdity.

PEDAL TECHNIQUE

The pedal keyboard on modern organs runs from CC to g; on older organs it extends only to f, and on older still only to d. On mediæval organs still in use in Europe it extends from D to d only.

Since pedal work demands a clean and sensitive pedal touch the organist should wear shoes which are as narrow as is consistent with perfect comfort, and made on a straight last so that the soles do not project. They should be of medium weight; too heavy shoes are unwieldy and interfere with the sensitiveness of the foot, while soles that are too thin are apt to overtire the more delicate foot muscles.

Before beginning practice it is well to glance at your organ pedals to make sure that they are clean, smooth, and slippery. You can no more do good work with muddy, sticky pedals than you could with molasses on your piano keys. Upon one occasion when Guilmant was playing at the Schola Cantorum, Paris, he seated himself on the organ bench, looked down at the pedals, got up and went out. The audience wondered greatly. In a few moments a man came in with a cloth and cleaned and polished the pedal keys, whereupon the great organist resumed his seat and began the recital.

When you have seated yourself in the middle of your organ bench put your feet down straight and close together, the left on C, the right on D. The feet should be flat on the keys. Some older instruction books direct the student to play with the tips of the toes; you have only to look at the shoes in the illustrations accompanying the directions in those books to see that this was the method of half a century ago, for which the too high organ bench was largely responsible. The foot should be flat on the key, the playing done on the ball of the foot.

The ankle movement corresponds to the wrist movement in manual technique, and most students will find their ankles amazingly stiff, as in ordinary life they do not seem to be used in such a manner as to make them as flexible as wrists usually are, and their flexibility has not been increased to the same extent by piano practice.

The relation of manual and pedal positions may be clearer if you will sit down in the position for playing, with the elbows close to the body, and take time to note how the arms from the elbows parallel the legs from the hips, and how the feet move from the ankles as the hands from the wrists. A certain amount of side-to-side movement is possible for the ankle without moving the leg, as it is for the wrist without moving the forearm; limbering up the ankles means simply acquiring that side-to-side movement.

The acquirement of correct and beautiful touch — and of the various touches — is as important for the pedals as for the manuals. In legato playing the student should strive to approach the degree of perfection demanded in finger legato. The principle is the same: the keys are *pressed*, not struck. When you play upon two keys in succession there will be one moment at which your first key ceases to sound, and a moment at which the second key begins to sound; legato playing means that these shall not be two different moments, but one and the same moment. Legato playing on the pedals is more difficult, for a beginner at least, than on the manuals.

Positions for Playing Intervals within an Octave

Do not look at the pedals during your pedal practice; be on your guard from the beginning against forming this habit. Put your knees together and acquire the following positions for the intervals, playing them legato — you only press the keys, you do not strike them. Be sure to keep your knees together. One well-known organist in Paris was obliged, as a student, to strap his knees together for a time when practising in order to fix the habit.

To play a Second:

Bring the feet together, touching. For example, when the left foot is on C and you want to make the right foot play D, bring it up until it clicks (noiselessly) against the left foot.

To play a Third:

Bring the feet together so that the ankles touch. Do not forget that your knees must *always* be held together.

To play a Fourth:

The heels touch and the ankle bones touch, with the toes turned out as far as possible.

To play a Fifth:

The knees must touch, and the heels, with the toes turned out as far as possible without strain.

To play an Octave:

The knees must be together and the feet turned out, separated, to what seems to be their greatest stretch at a natural angle without any straining.

The Fourth, Fifth, and Octave — the Subdominant, Dominant, Tonic — are the most important positions, as of the most frequent occurrence.

The remaining intervals are found from those already acquired.

To play a Sixth:

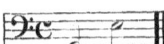

Take the position for a Fifth and play the next note above.

To play a Seventh:

Assume the position for the Octave and play the next note below. These two intervals are always the hardest to play, just as they are the most difficult in sight-singing, in which they are found in exactly the same way.

This takes care of everything up to the Octave; it is easy to find one over the Octave, in the same manner as one below. A step greater than this is rare in simpler music, in hymns, simple anthems, and vocal accompanying, and by the time the student reaches the more elaborate he will be sufficiently at home on all parts of the keyboard to put his foot anywhere, at will.

Sufficient practice with this system will fix the intervals so that you will not need to look at the pedal keyboard any more than you do at the manuals. Nor will you need to fall back upon other aids sometimes suggested, such as always verifying your notes by first touching the nearest black note. Do not allow yourself to yield to this weakness; indulgence in it destroys your confidence. One who has taught many organists realizes how many are veritable slaves to this "black note habit."

LEGATO TOUCH ON THE PEDALS

Legato touch on the pedals is obtained in four ways:
I. With alternate feet;   II. With toe and heel;   III. Glissando;   IV. Substitution.

In scale playing we start with the general principle that the first five notes of the scale are played with the left foot, the other three with the right foot. Naturally, this principle is modified as more and more black notes enter. To play the scale of C, for example: beginning with the left foot, when the toe depresses C raise the heel just enough to move it over on top of D; then depress the heel, raising the toe barely enough to slide over D to the top of E. Do not raise toe or heel any higher than is absolutely necessary; remember that you do not strike the note, but press it with the side of the sole, the ball of the foot, with the same character of touch as that employed in legato playing on the manuals.

Do not forget that when the right foot comes up to take its first note it must click (noiselessly) against the left in order to make sure of striking the correct note cleanly; it will blur if the right foot is not tight against the left.

∧ above the note signifies right toe, ∧ below the note signifies left toe.
U above the note signifies right heel, U below the note signifies left heel.

In other scales, when you are about to pass from a white key to a black key the heel on the white key must be just near enough the black key to permit of depressing the black key with the toe. When playing on white and black keys alternately play a little farther in on the keyboard than when playing on white keys only.

When a foot has finished playing a note, leave it lightly where it is, conveniently at hand for its next note. Do not put it away back under the bench so that it will take a long time to bring it in from a distance when you need it again.

In the D major scale we find the first exception to the general rule of pedaling, as a black key occurs in the first five notes, namely F♯; this is taken out by the right foot, the other four notes only being played by the left foot. Otherwise proceed as before.

Beginning with this D major scale it is necessary to be especially watchful that the knees are kept together, and the feet also, very closely. This will make the work not only more exact, but easier as well. So in the scale of E the feet march along side by side touching each other all the time.

PEDAL GLISSANDO

When the scale of B is reached a new procedure is demanded to permit of passing legato from F♯ to G♯ in the ascending scale, A♯ to G♯ descending. This is *glissando*, which may, therefore, fitly be considered here.

Glissando on the pedal is used with frequency in four fields, namely in passing: (1) from a black key to a white; (2) from a black key to a black; (3) from a white key to a white; (4) from a white key to a black.

(1) In passing from a black key to a white, as in this passage for the right foot:

the only way to play legato is to slide from C♯ to D with the toe; this gives you the heel for E, and the toe in position to play the F♯. Incidentally, you must guard against too much clatter of the keys.

(2) In moving from a black key to another black key advance "toeing in," if possible, up with the left foot, down with the right, as this gives you better control of the keys. If the action of the organ is absolutely noiseless, or, frequently, when you are playing full organ, you can slide from one note to the other on the outer edge of the sole of the foot; otherwise, play the first black note with the outer side of the shoe and the second black note with the inner side, moving it over by throwing the heel in quickly:

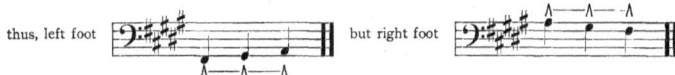

Occasionally it is necessary to advance "toeing out," instead, as in octave runs when both feet are busy:

(3) and (4) Passing from a white key to a white or from a white key to a black is demanded only in glissando runs, as described at the end of this chapter.

SUBSTITUTION

Another aid to legato playing which is as indispensable to pedal as to manual technique is Substitution. This is of two kinds: I. Substitution of one foot for another; II. Exchange of heel and toe of the same foot.

I. Substitution of one foot for another is necessary to maintain the legato when two extended melodic skips occur in immediate succession, as:

Play low C with the left toe, second C with the right heel, well forward on the key; substitute left toe for right heel and play high C with right toe. Only so can this be played legato. Always, if possible, substitute a heel for a toe, or a toe for a heel; if the heel is placed well forward on the key and the toe of the other foot back of it, there will be no danger of tripping.

II. Exchange of heel and toe of the same foot.

When you find yourself in a position which demands that a white key shall be followed by a black, and for some good and sufficient reason you have played the white key with the toe, it becomes necessary to substitute the heel for the toe on that white key in order that the toe may be set free to play the black key without interrupting the legato.

This form of substitution is frequently overdone; organists will sometimes play down a whole scale in this manner. It is well to avoid unnecessary and superfluous use of it, as it can establish itself as a sort of nervous habit.

There is no reason that can be accepted as adequate for breaking the legato in any piece or passage which should be played legato. When, for instance, you are playing an expressive melody and your right foot is occupied with the Swell pedal, do not imagine that you have in this any excuse for permitting the left foot to play a legato passage roughly, or staccato; you can maintain the perfect legato with the left foot, and that not merely in playing adjacent keys, but thirds, fourths, and fifths.

When playing a sixth, or anything larger, which the left foot cannot compass alone, bring the right foot down from the **Swell** pedal for the one extra note; see "Pedal Etude in A," Alkan, in Part II, Section XX.

Playing Skips of a Third

In order to play thirds on the white keys legato, as in such a passage as

when the right toe depresses middle C swing the heel over D to E, turning the foot slightly in order to have the full benefit of its arch in avoiding D; then use the heel which is depressing E as a pivot on which to swing the toe over F to G; then use the toe which is depressing G as a pivot to swing the heel over A to B.

Sequential Pedaling

A point of general importance in pedaling, as indeed in manual technique as well, is to take care that when sequential passages occur in the music the pedaling — or fingering — shall be sequential also. Even though there may be some awkward spots it is worth while to persist in this as it is much easier and more satisfactory in the end.

Extended Pedal Glissando

Extended pedal glissando has been made possible by the modern pedal keyboard. When it is necessary to execute a run on the white notes of the pedals with the right foot, draw the foot rapidly over the keys, playing on the ball of the foot if moving up the keyboard, on the outer side if moving down. Reverse this procedure for the left foot.

When this run includes both black and white notes, as the scale of E♭, for example,

pull the foot with heel first E♭ to D, D to C, movements with which you are already familiar; at C turn the foot with the toe *in* and play *up* on the black note B♭. A♭, G, F, call for only familiar movements; then toe in again and play *up* on E♭. In passing from a white key to a black in a glissando run it is necessary always to raise the toe sufficiently to permit it to slide up on the black key from the white, pulling the foot in and out in order to reach the keys. This is, of course, impossible on an old-fashioned, straight, stiff keyboard.

Going back up the scale of E♭ the movements will be reversed: E♭, F, G, are played pulling the heel first with the toe turned in; to reach A♭ turn the foot around, with the toe *out* slide to B♭; turn the heel out and slide to C and D with the toe in; slide to E♭ with the heel in, toe out.

Sometimes in such runs, as in the scale of E major, for example, it will be found advantageous to effect the glissando on the white notes with the heel; see Part II, Section XX.

Touches other than Legato

The other organ touches besides the legato, namely, I. Non-legato, Semi-detached, or Brillante; II. Marcato; III. Staccato, are employed on the pedal as on the manuals, in the same kinds of passages and with the same effects. They are controlled from the ankle. Studies in these touches will be found in Part II, Sections X, XI.

Pedal Scales

a) Pedal Alone
b) Pedal with Manuals

The Major Scales for Pedal

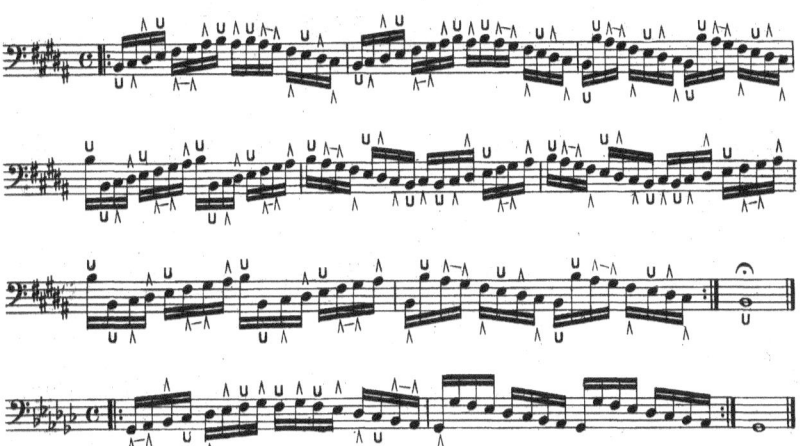

The student should fill out the exercise on each scale according to the plan of those preceding.

The Harmonic Minor Scales for Pedal

The Melodic Minor Scales for Pedal

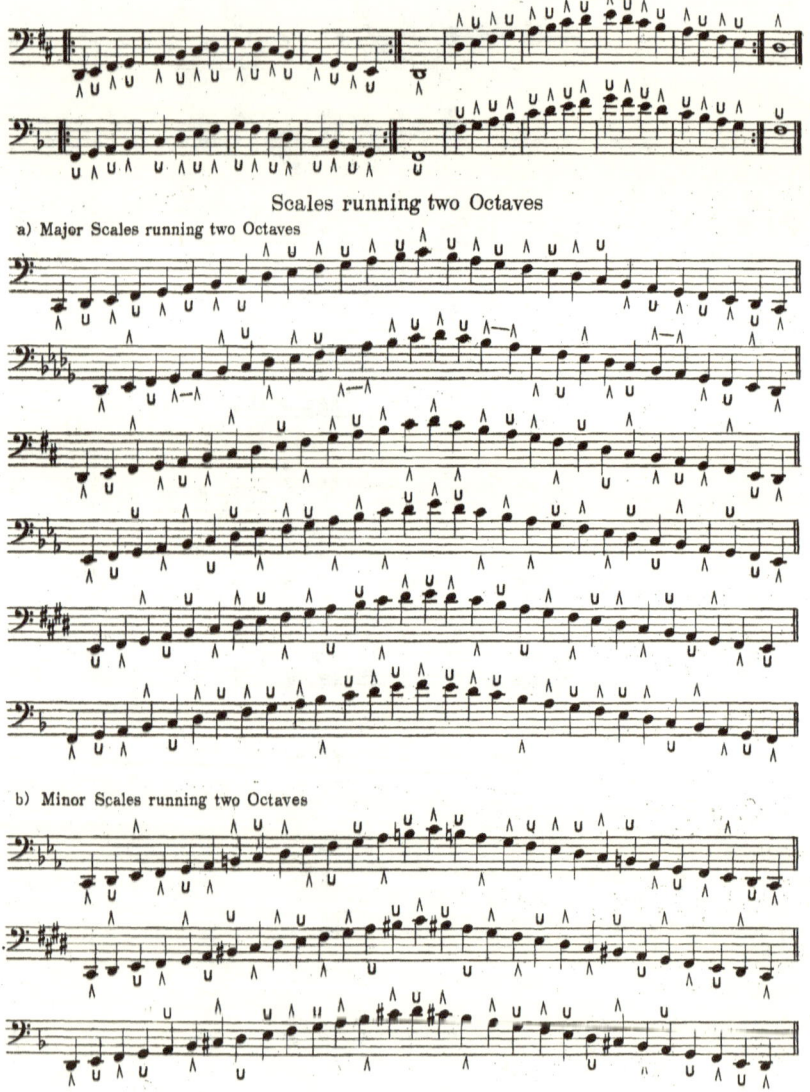

Scale passages

The pedalling of the following should be marked by the student.

Sw: Diapasons
Ped: Violone, Bd. 16′, 8′,

Allegretto

Sw. Bd. 16′, Strs, Sw. to Sw. 16′, Sw. to Gt. 16′, 8′
Gt. Diap. II, Fl's, 8′, 4′
Ped. Diap. II, Violone 16′, Bd. 16′, 8′, Sw. to Ped.

THE PEDALS AND THEIR EMPLOYMENT

By the Pedals (from the Latin *pes*, a foot; or, perhaps more correctly, from *pedalis*, of or belonging to the feet) is here signified that special department of the organ, invented by Bernard the German about 1450, of which the keyboard, having a compass of something over two octaves, is played with the feet, and has keys of a shape suited to this purpose. The true function of the pedals is to supply to the manuals an independent or obbligato bass part.

To employ the pedals, in season and out of season, as a mere strengthening part, to make them serve a base and homophonic drudgery, by doubling the manual bass in the octave below, is such a misuse, and shows such poverty of invention, that it ought to be avoided in all good organ-music, though the modern exponents of extempore playing resort to it only too often; there are, it is true, some occasions when this use of the pedals is impressive and quite justified, but these occur only in accompaniments, especially in those of masses, chorales, hymns, and the like; never, or very rarely, in polyphony or in independent organ-music. Excellent guidance in this matter has been furnished us in the works of Buxtehude, Bach, Händel, Albrechtsberger, and many others. Unfortunately, the poor, starved, homophonic use of the pedals has had a similar influence on the art of organ-building, insomuch that builders have been led to adopt the equally poor, starved "coupling-pedals," which tend considerably to hinder the progress of sound organ-playing. It is to be hoped that improved pedal technique, honest playing and contrapuntal training will before long effect the abolition of coupling-pedals in favor of the independent pedal organ.

GENERAL EXPLANATION

The student is advised not to accompany his pedal exercises in unison on the manual, as experience shows that this form of practising is not to be recommended.

To acquire at the same time certainty in attack and rapid execution, every note played by a foot not previously engaged should be struck with the foot parallel to the key, as shown in the following diagram; and it is most important that the angular movements of the feet, both from heel and toe, should be made in conformity with the diagonal lines marked across the pedals, those in Fig. 1 being for intervals of a second, and those in Fig. 2 for thirds. The marks for the left foot are placed below the staff; those for the right foot, above it.

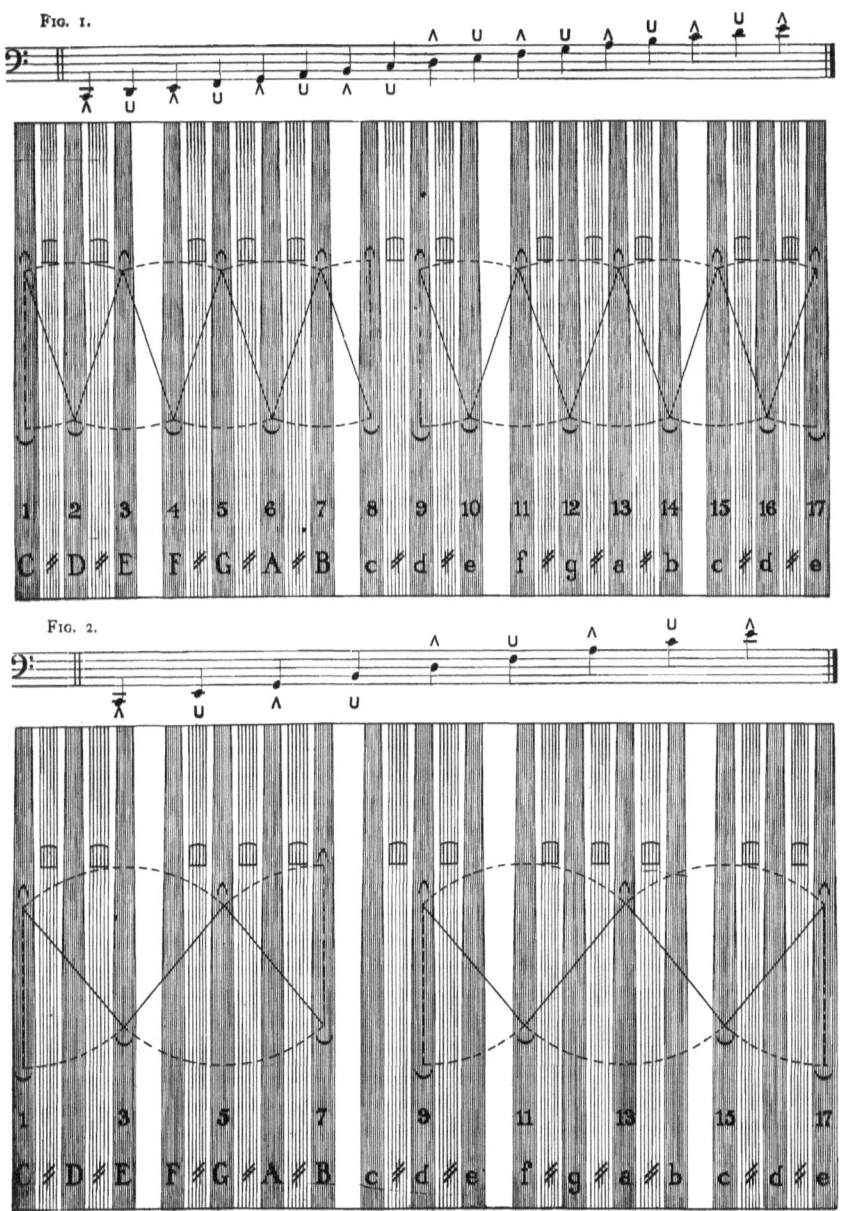

The difference between the angles through which the foot moves, in the intervals of a second and a third respectively, renders it plainly necessary to practise each of them separately with extreme strictness, taking great care that the angular movements (especially the more difficult) are performed slowly at first, but with unfailing correctness, in accordance with the positions indicated by the diagonal lines in the above drawings; and the student must work thus through the given exercises in progressive order; the pace may afterwards be gradually increased.

These angular movements for seconds and thirds, when combined in the same passage, form so important a part of the student's technique, that we here present several specimen diagrams, demonstrating to the eye the nature of this class of difficulty. Thus, in Fig. 3, *A* shows the appearance which a passage will bear when the first note is played with the toe; *B* gives the reversed appearance of the same figure, when the passage of notes printed below is commenced with the heel; while the more elaborate figure at *C* illustrates a more complex design produced by the mixture of seconds and thirds. The reverse of this figure *C* might be produced by beginning the passage with the heel, as *A* is reversed at *B*. In performing these mixed passages of seconds and thirds, the feet reach several different positions, some more forward on the keys, some farther back, owing to the different size of the arc traversed in executing the various intervals. In *A* and *B* two such different positions are reached; in *C* three, the third position being the farthest back.

FIG. 3.

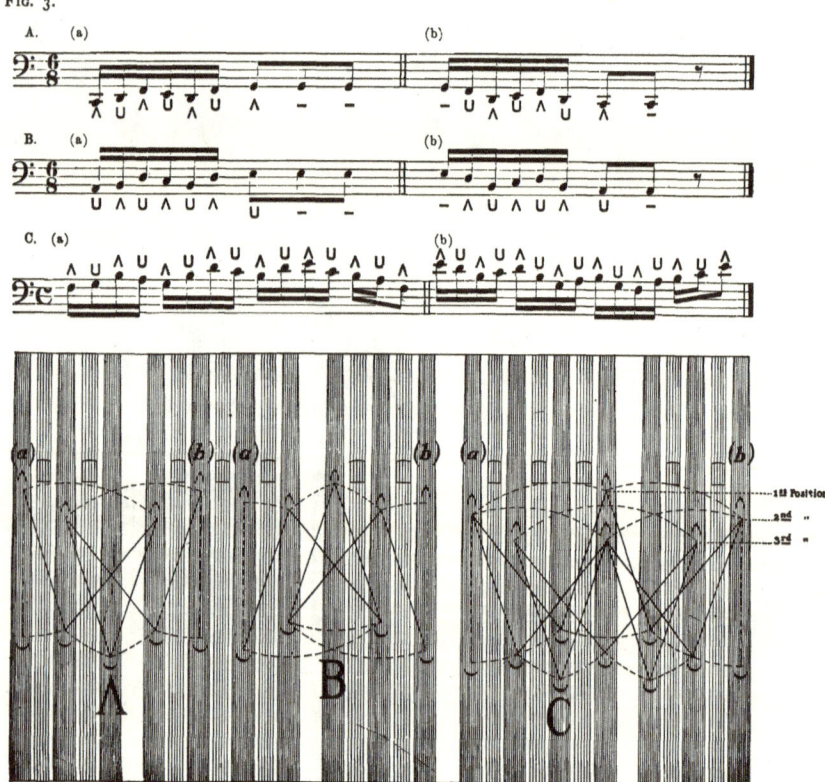

Special attention must be paid to such sequences as those in Fig. 4 (which rarely occur except when playing in octaves), on account of the shifting of position which they involve. Fig. *A* shows the impossibility of carrying out such a passage without sliding the foot along the key; while *B* shows how this sliding is to be effected. And here also the figure will assume a reversed appearance if the passage is commenced with the toe instead of the heel.

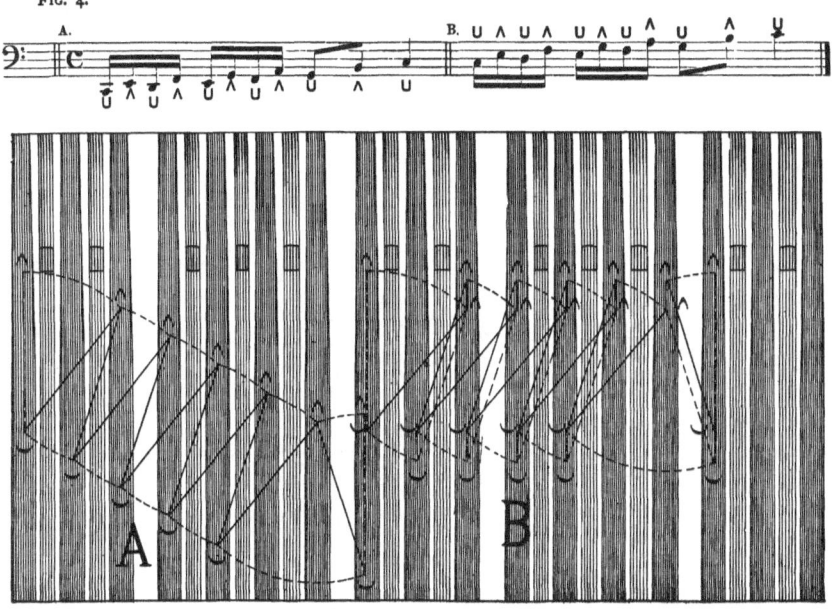

Fig. 4.

On all keyed instruments there are certain steps from one key to another which are the same in size, though the musical intervals they represent may be different; this is seen in Figs. 5 and 6. Since the feet, unlike the hands, cannot enlarge or diminish their stretch, it follows that more importance attaches to observing the actual size of steps on the pedals than on the manuals.

FIG. 5.

Compare the printed notes with the pedal diagrams.

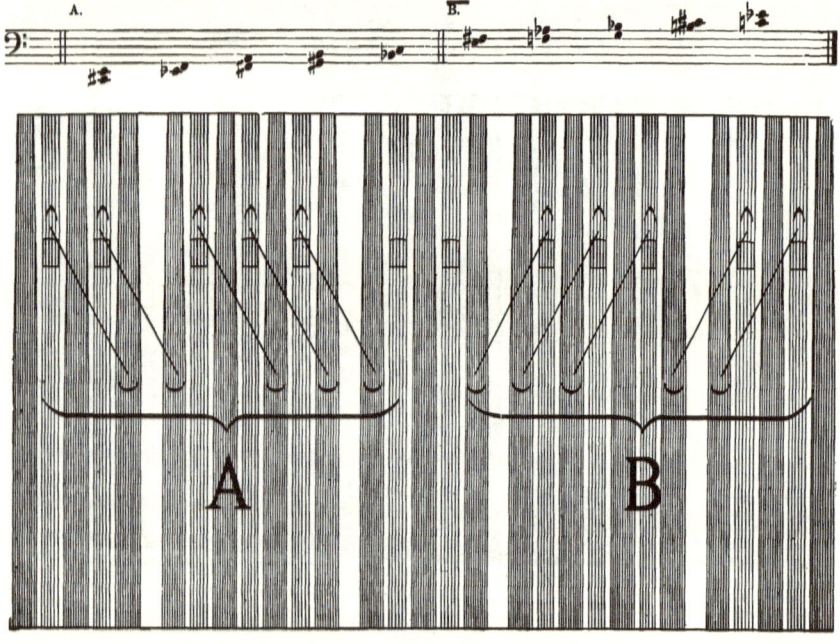

FIG. 6.

Compare the printed notes with the pedal diagrams.

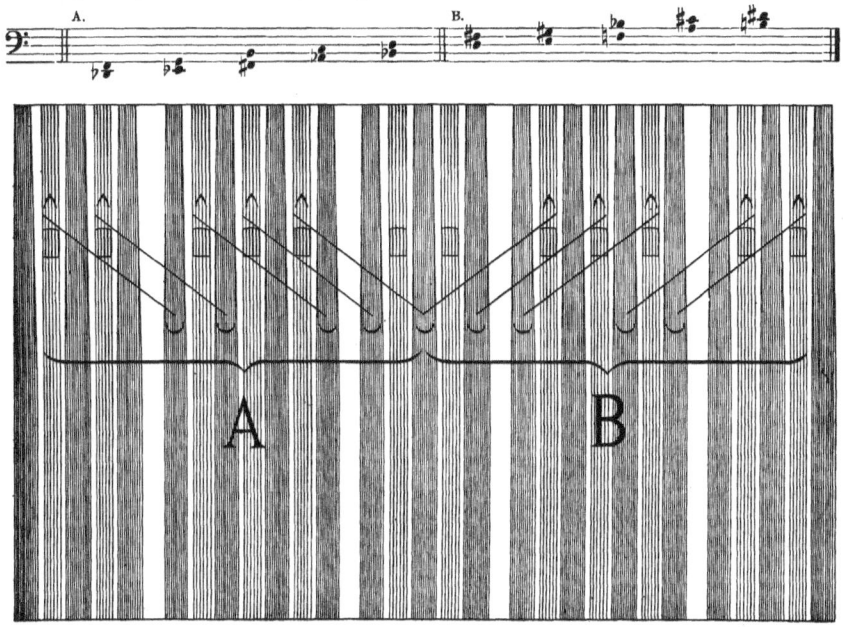

In the pedal diagrams in Figs. 7, 8, 9, 10, are shown the movements of the feet in similar arpeggios in different keys. It must, however, be remarked that the example in Fig. 8 cannot well be executed on the pedal-boards now in use, since their construction, as before observed, is not adapted for perfectly systematic pedal-playing.

A comparison in each case of the notes with the pedal diagram will show the importance of the latter to the student of technique.

FIG. 7.

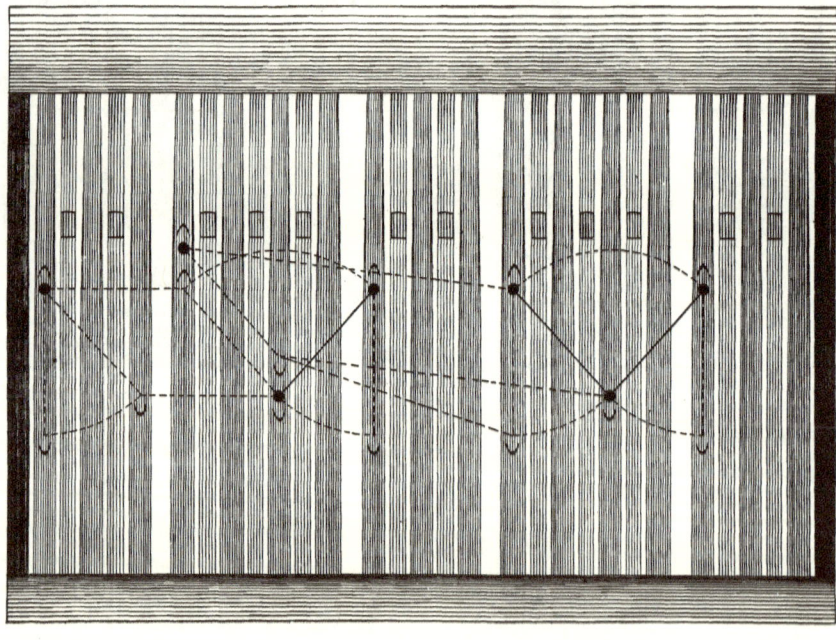

Fig. 8.

Fig. 9.

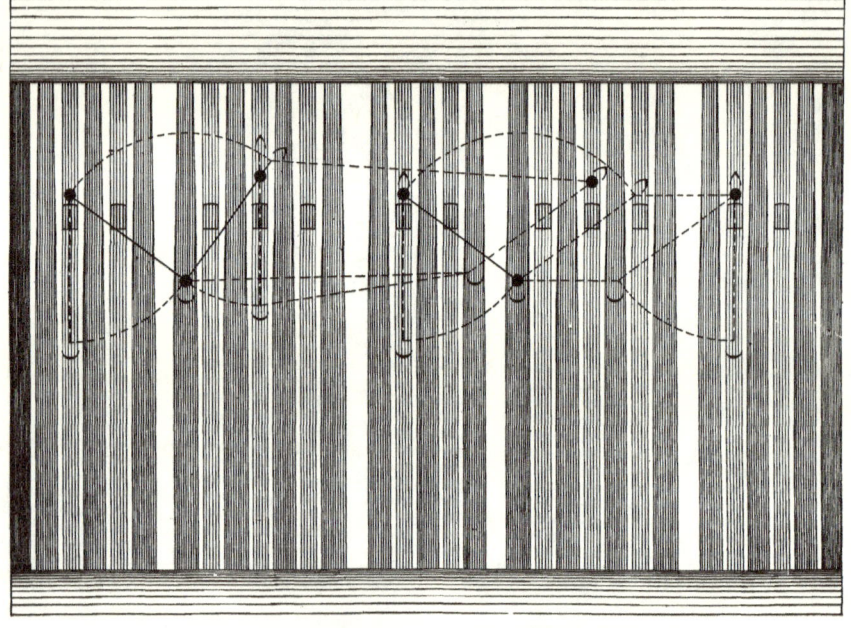

Many more explanations of the same character, which must be omitted here, are nevertheless of such value, that a future generation, more interested in the subject, will doubtless work them out and accord them due attention; but the examples given above will furnish a clear and distinct indication of the principles of a scientifically built-up pedal technique.

To keep the movements of the feet as small and as natural as possible is the first and most important condition of ready execution on the pedals.

EXPLANATION OF THE EXERCISES

SECTION I

A. Exercises in Diatonic Seconds, for Each Foot Alone

In these exercises, from No. 1 to No. 12 inclusive, the toe strikes the accented notes; and the exercises should be practised again, with the heel on the notes previously struck by the toe.

B. Exercises with Notes Repeated on an Accent

Exercises 13 to 18 include repeated notes, which the beginner is apt to strike noisily; this mistake must be corrected, and the exercises performed with such suppleness as to avoid making a clatter on the keys, and also to connect the notes into a satisfactory legato.

C. Exercises in which the Foot Advances by Taking a New Position

The exercises from No. 18 to No. 24 include repeated notes on which the foot advances into a new position. After each group of notes under a slur the foot is to be considered free; hence, the next note is to be struck with the foot parallel to the key, and only afterwards must the foot be turned sideways. These exercises, like those under *A*, must be repeated with the places of heel and toe reversed.

D. Exercises in Diatonic Thirds, for Each Foot Alone

These must be treated like the preceding exercises. It must be remarked that pedal practice demands shoes with specially light soles, and that heels of the French type, which are under the middle of the foot, are out of the question when performing such exercises as these.

The constant habit among beginners of commencing a passage with the foot diagonally across the keys has to be frequently corrected by the teacher. The attack with the foot askew is very seldom called for in passages for one foot alone; though in passages for both feet, the straight and the skew positions may both be used in turn with full justification, as will be explained later.

E. Exercises on Mixed Seconds and Thirds, for Each Foot Alone

In several of these exercises the foot has to slide a little in order to keep it in a middle position (see Fig. 3). The backward movement of the foot may, however, in a few cases be allowed to extend even to the third position on the long keys. Such exceptional cases as are shown in Figs. 7 and 9 (above) do not apply, as regards the position of the feet and the attack with the toe askew, to exercises like the present.

F. Chromatic Exercises for Each Foot Alone

The sliding motion which occurs in these exercises is from the sloping end of the sharp key to the next following natural key. Even here the correct design of the pedals is of importance; for if the sharp keys are cut off square at the end, the keys are more likely to rattle than if their ends are sloped. If the pedals are carefully bushed with felt, and their surfaces are even and smoothly polished, it will be highly conducive to noiseless execution and easy sliding from one key to another.

SECTION II

A. Exercises for Both Feet Together

The aim of these exercises in contrary motion with varied footing is partly to promote increased facility in what was acquired previously, and at the same time to prepare the way for what is to follow.

It is especially important that these exercises should not be laid aside until a rapid tempo has been attained with every variety of footing.

B. Solid and Broken Octaves

A difficulty occurs here which is not so easily surmounted as might be supposed at first sight. For here, as in all octave-playing on the pedals, the rule holds good without exception, that the first attack of the feet, and the subsequent side-movements, must be symmetrical and simultaneous. In other words, whether the heels move or the toes, they must at all points in the arc which they describe keep precisely the same distance between them. This rule applies not only to exercises in solid or simultaneous octaves, but in a still higher degree to those in broken octaves; for by this method of practice, conscientiously carried out, the student may acquire a technical facility which will exceed all his expectations. The same rules apply equally to thirds and sixths, both broken and solid.

To ensure retaining the regularity of the motions of the feet when playing broken intervals, it is recommended that the student go through the solid intervals of the same kind every second or third time, and pay good heed that the angular movements of the feet are simultaneous in the broken no less than in the solid intervals.

The student is advised to do his utmost to secure a true legato; such a legato, that is, as results from pressing every key down to its full extent, and joining every sound in the legato phrase closely to the next one. There is another kind of legato, which may be called a light legato, which floats, as it were, on the top of the keys, and results in pressing them only halfway down; and it is much to be deplored that this half-legato, which produces an inferior tone from the organ, has often become a deeply rooted habit, under lazy and thoughtless teaching. Without a firm legato, true organ-playing becomes inconceivable.

It is likewise to be observed that the student, before he has mastered a true legato, manifests at first a tendency to hold the accented notes beyond their proper length; this error is illustrated in full in the following example:

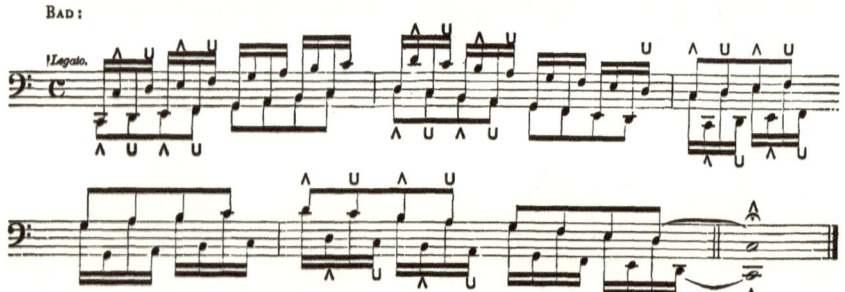

whereas, when the above fault has been corrected, the passage will regain its original appearance, as shown below:

The absolute superiority of the method proposed in the present work over the older ones does not lie in the construction of the exercises so much as in the manner of practising them. The one aim of the technical directions given in the whole of this Part is to attain, by means of the smallest and most natural movements, to a smooth execution, to accuracy, to rapidity, and to a true legato.

SECTION III

This Section, which consists of free adaptations from the previous one, attempts to show how and when deviations from the previous rules may be allowed.

Such a case occurs in Ex. *A* 3, an exception in footing, inasmuch as the feet move on one degree to a new position before they find it necessary to use any angular motion. That this movement is an advantageous exception to the rule can be proved experimentally by a thorough trial of both methods.

When the pupil reaches Exs. 15 and 16, he will find further proofs of the wisdom of such exceptional footings, though they by no means invalidate the general application of the original rule.

In *B* there likewise occur footings which involve a mixture of angular motion with change of position; and Exs. *C*, Nos. 27, 28, 29, are planned for acquiring accuracy in moving the whole foot onwards. Here the pupil is apt to swing his feet about needlessly, a fault which calls for correction.

In Exs. 30, 31 occurs mixed legato and staccato, in conjunction with a mixed footing partly of angular motion and partly of moving the whole foot. The staccato must, like all organ staccato, be so performed that the keys are pressed down as far as they will go, and the legato (as before mentioned) must be a true legato.

Section *D* consists entirely of exercises for changing the feet on one key, in passages both of single and double notes; the clearness of such passages, however, depends much upon the proper construction of the pedal-board. Such exercises are intended merely for the improvement of execution, for no good organ-music would contain passages like these.

SECTION IV

A. Major Scales

The footing of these, as well as of the minor scales, is, in the main, the same as that employed by J. Lemmens in his Organ-School; but since the pedal scales in the present work have been considerably extended in length by varying their outlines, in order that the pupil might not lay them aside too soon, it has been found necessary to modify the footing in several places.

It will, therefore, be both useful and necessary to give a few analytical demonstrations of those alterations of footing which have been suggested by experience as conducive to improved technique, together with some remarks on the footing of scales in general.

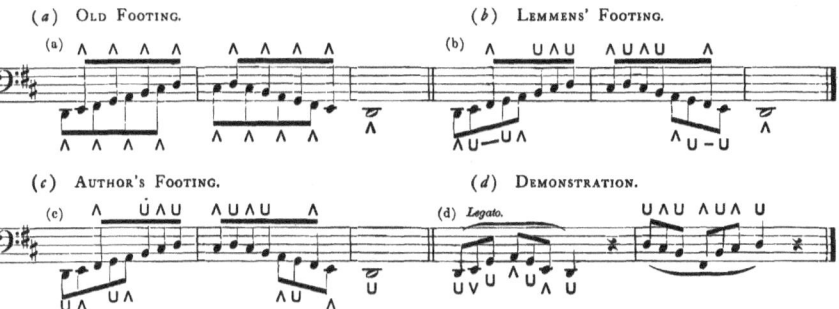

That the footing at (*a*) has come to be regarded as a mere solecism in the light of our ideas, is due to Lemmens and the reform founded by him upon truth and nature; for, had it not been for this pioneer of truth, the adepts in the old double-shuffle footing might have rested content with their unintelligent method for a long time to come. Lemmens' footing is shown at (*b*) and the author's at (*c*).

The footing at (*c*), which provides for a strict legato not only for the scale in its entirety, but also for the part played by each foot separately, as shown at (*d*), is alone adapted for rapid execution.

As another example of the improved footing, the scale of B flat major is given:

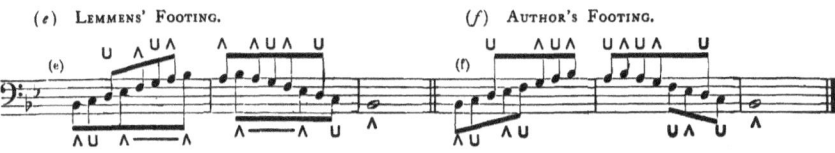

(The old footing is not given, as being altogether impracticable.)

75

(g) DEMONSTRATION.

(h) DEMONSTRATION.

Lemmens' footing is shown at (*e*) and the author's at (*f*).

The footing at (*f*) is not only calculated for strict legato, as proved at (*g*), but also affords variety in scale-practice, as shown in the examples at (*h*).

Having adopted a certain form of scale-passage as the normal formula for practice in all keys alike, we have next to determine the footing for each scale as framed on this formula; but the footing will be subject to partial modification in cases where the scale is altered or extended so as to differ from the formula, as in the following example:

(*i*) NORMAL SCALE-FORMULA.

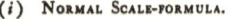

(*k*) DEMONSTRATION.

(*l*) EXTENDED SCALE.

(*m*) DEMONSTRATION.

Both in scales and in other melodic passages, that footing is to be preferred which will give the closest legato for the separate part played by each foot; and this should be, for every thoughtful pupil, the universal principle on which to base a reliable pedal-technique.

There is one other movement of the foot, which has been purposely left till the last; namely, gliding from one sharp key to the next. These gliding movements must be practised in such a way that the attack on the second key, on to which we glide, is, if possible, made as firmly as any other attack. Sliding movements of this kind are, in spite of the most diligent practice, always uncertain in rapid passages. An improved construction of the pedals is the only means by which they could be rendered superfluous.*

B. Melodic Minor Scales

The technical principles of construction and footing in these scales is in the main the same as in the major, and thus a description of them is superfluous.

C. Harmonic Minor Scales

As the independent nature of these scales is much contested, the author intends to avoid entering into any details concerning them but such as bear upon Technique; in this respect these scales are well worthy of consideration.

That the pupil may accustom himself to the recognized form of this scale, all accidental chromatic signs are omitted, and are replaced throughout, in the signature, by those which by themselves proclaim the construction of the scale.

In conclusion, the author feels bound to exhort the student who seeks to progress in pedal-playing, by help of these studies, to ponder carefully the above technical rules and demonstrations, that he may, by means of them, and still more by the use of his own intellect, become master of a method eminently based upon nature and upon scientific truth; for the exercises alone will not suffice, since these present only a series of passages for practice with marks for footing, but do not teach how to practise the passages to advanta ;e.

---

* TRANSLATOR'S NOTE.—This "gliding" is performed as follows: While the foot is on the first key, raise slightly that side of the foot which is nearest to the second key; then, if the pedals are as smooth as they should be, it is easy to slide the foot from one to the other.

A FEW WORDS ON THE MUSICAL EDUCATION OF ORGAN STUDENTS

The student who is gifted with musical talent and a turn for playing the organ, and who wishes to train himself in that art, must as early as possible work through the most important pianoforte studies, and only after this may proceed to the special study on the organ of the grand style of music which belongs to that sublime instrument, for which no piano studies, even those of the most general application, are sufficient.

It will be of great use to the intending organ pupil, if his future study of the organ is so far taken into account that, during the latter part of his pianoforte studies, his teacher on that instrument will give the preference to work in the polyphonic style.

This, however, is only that he may understand and become habituated to the independent motion of parts which belongs to polyphonic music; it is by no means advisable (though we find it done occasionally) to practise organ-music on the piano, making use of the strict legato, the substitution of fingers and other characteristics which are called for only on the manuals of the organ.

Pianoforte-playing must on the one side preserve its genuine independent style as much as organ-playing on the other; especially as the organist, for economic reasons, is often forced to rely more on the former than on the latter.

Since it is the privilege of the organist more than of any other musician to be the exponent of the majestic Fugue to a public whose musical culture is ever increasing, it is only reasonable that these expounders of fugue should, during their student days, enjoy a thorough course of instruction in harmony, counterpoint, canon, and fugue, and should diligently apply themselves thereto. The organist with whom this knowledge is lacking can never turn to full account his technical powers, however great they may be; while his conception of his music, if he lacks musical scholarship, can never show a spark of ideality.

Besides the technical and scientific training which is demanded by the organ, with its elaborate and scholastic style of music, the student must also make a study of his grand instrument itself; and this must by no means confine itself to a mere knowledge of the pitch of stops as reckoned in feet, their qualities, titles, and powers alone or in combination; but must extend to the construction, action, and material of the pipes, the windchest, the reservoirs, bellows, windtrunks, couplers, and pneumatics both of manual and pedal, both of draw-stop action and key-action.

Every organ candidate who is thoroughly equipped in the above subjects possesses a musical education which will make him a credit to the institution which grants him his degree. Such a player may rightly be placed in charge of a really fine organ; for the art of which he is master will return a full reward to the congregation which honors him with an appointment.

Part II.
Section I.
Exercises for Each Foot Alone.
A. Long Trills.

B. Exercises with notes repeated on an accent.

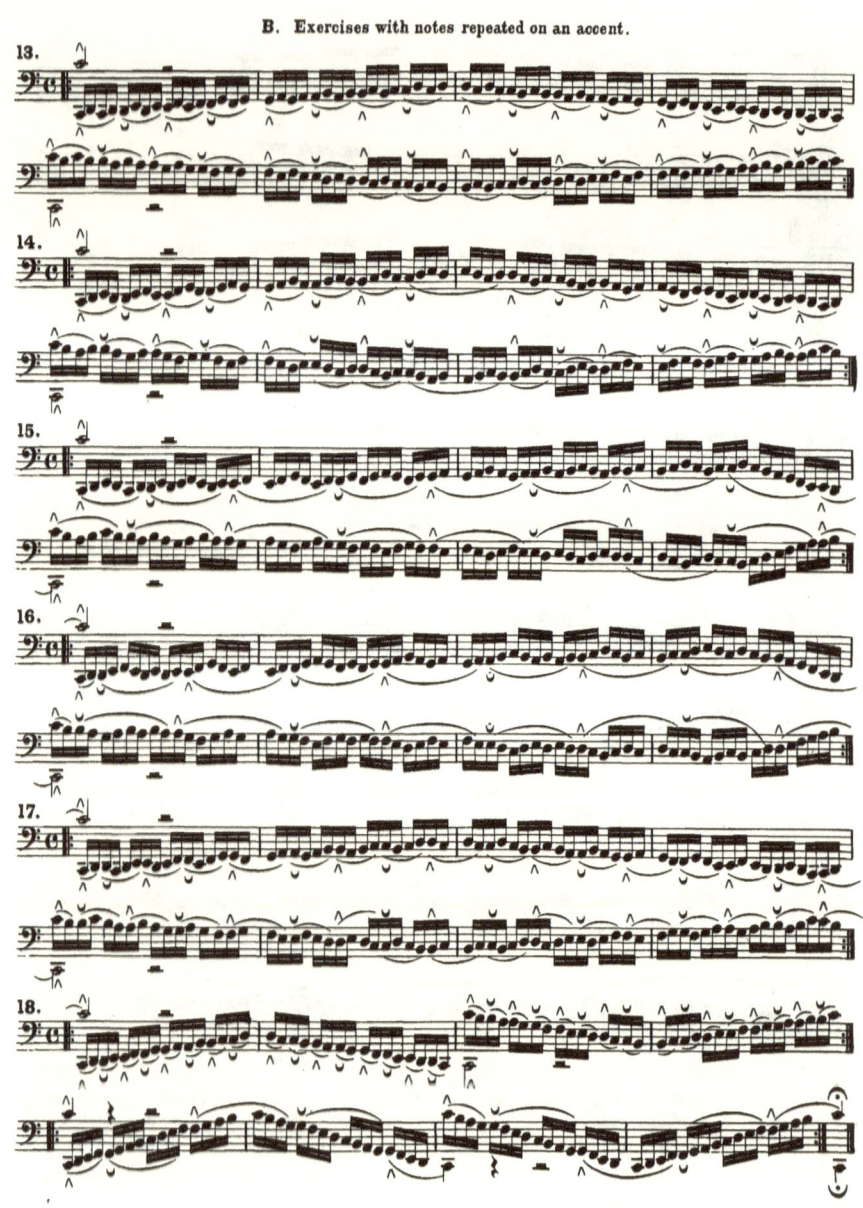

C. Exercises in which the foot advances by taking a new position.

D. Exercises in Diatonic Thirds.

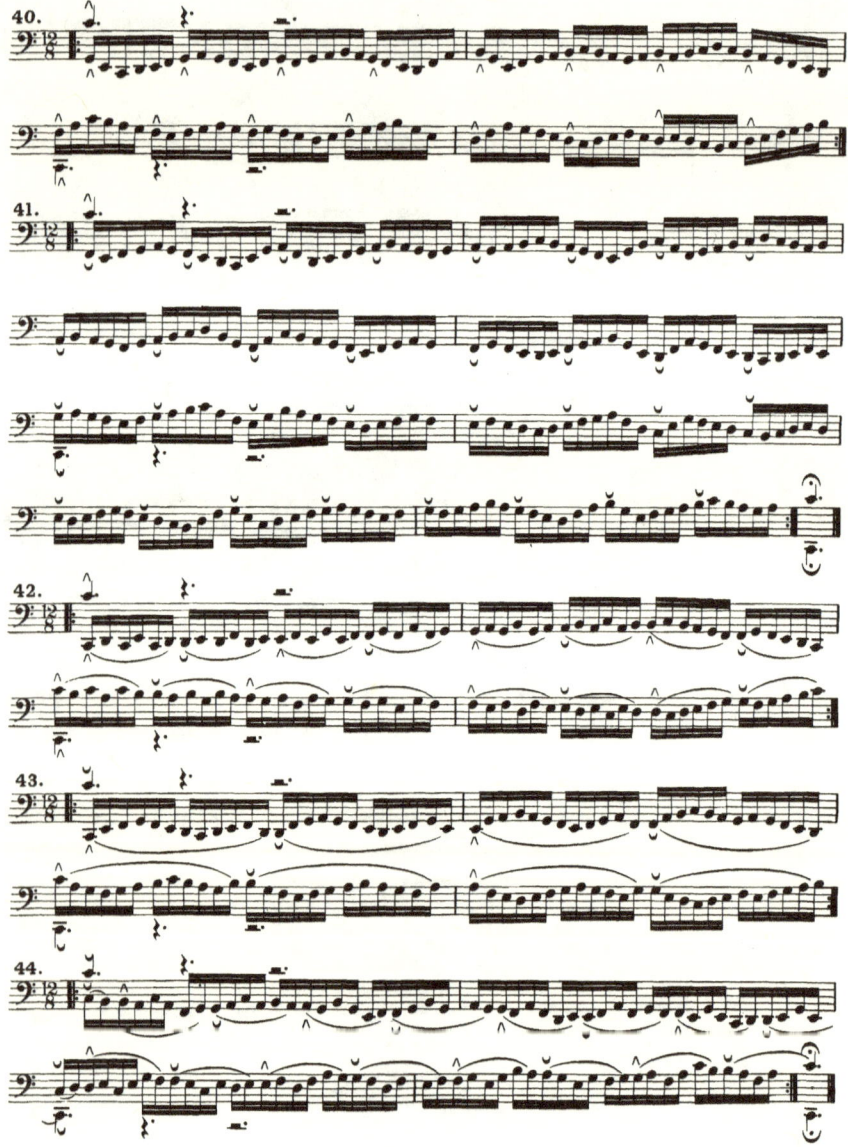

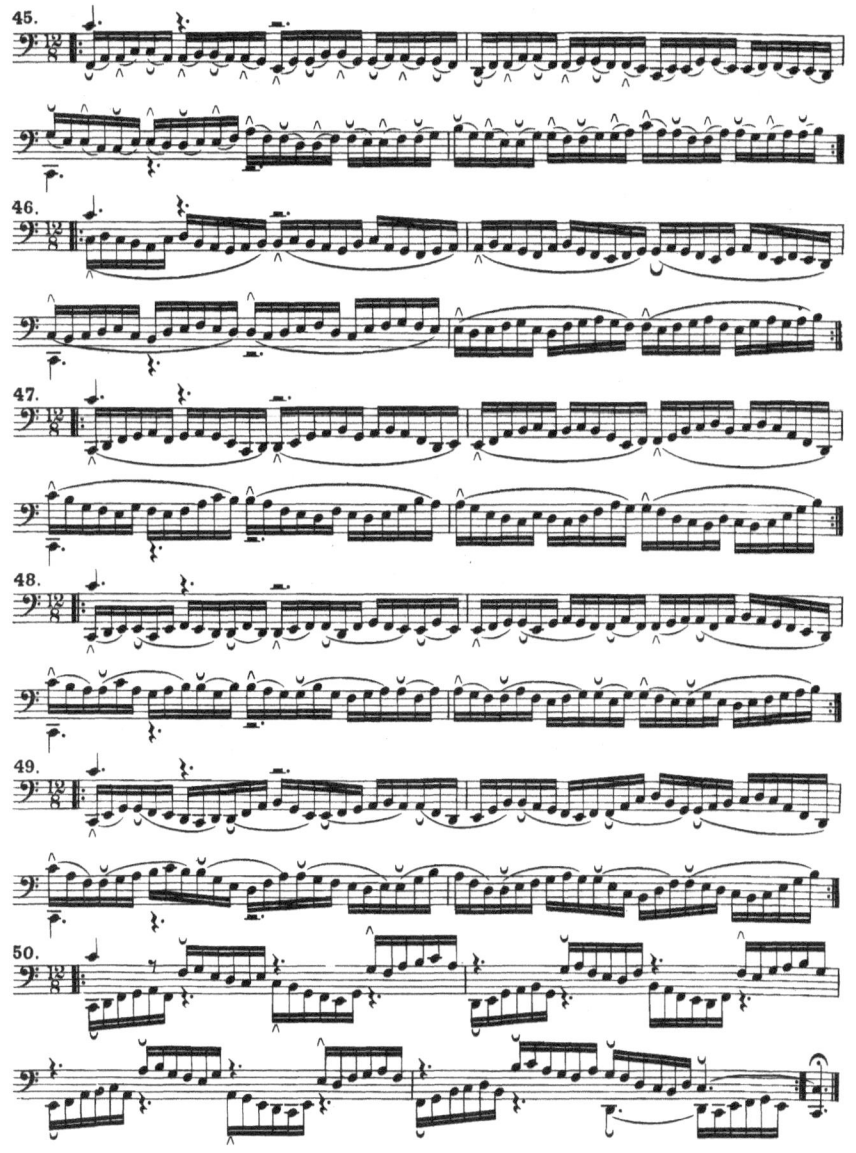

F. Chromatic Exercises.

Section II.
A. Exercises for Both Feet Together.

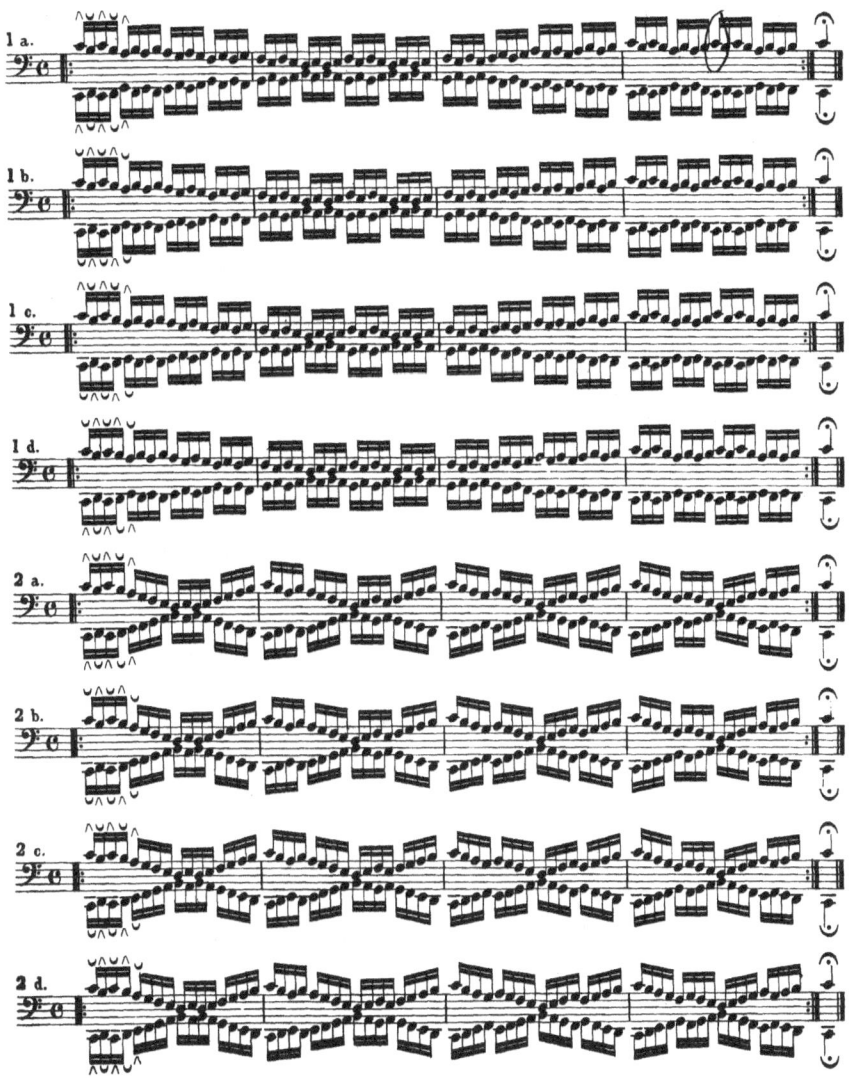

B. Double-Pedalling in Octaves.

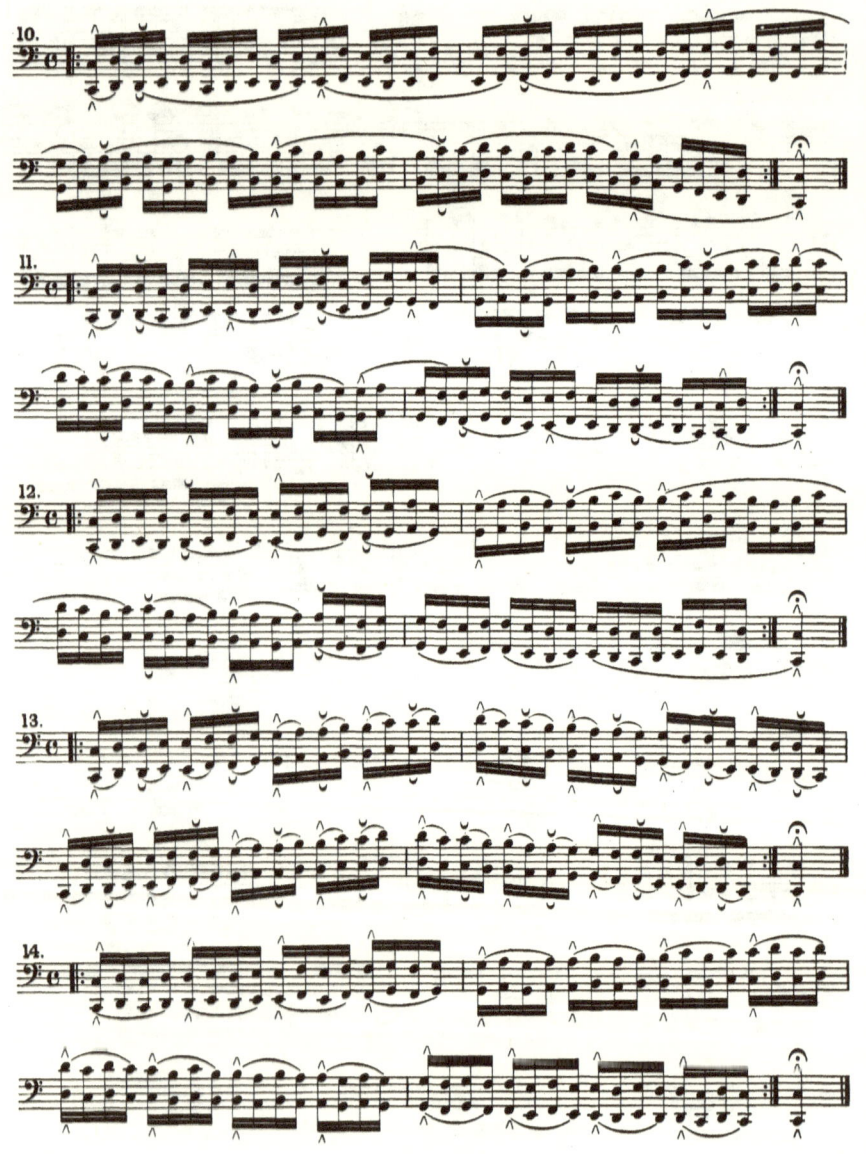

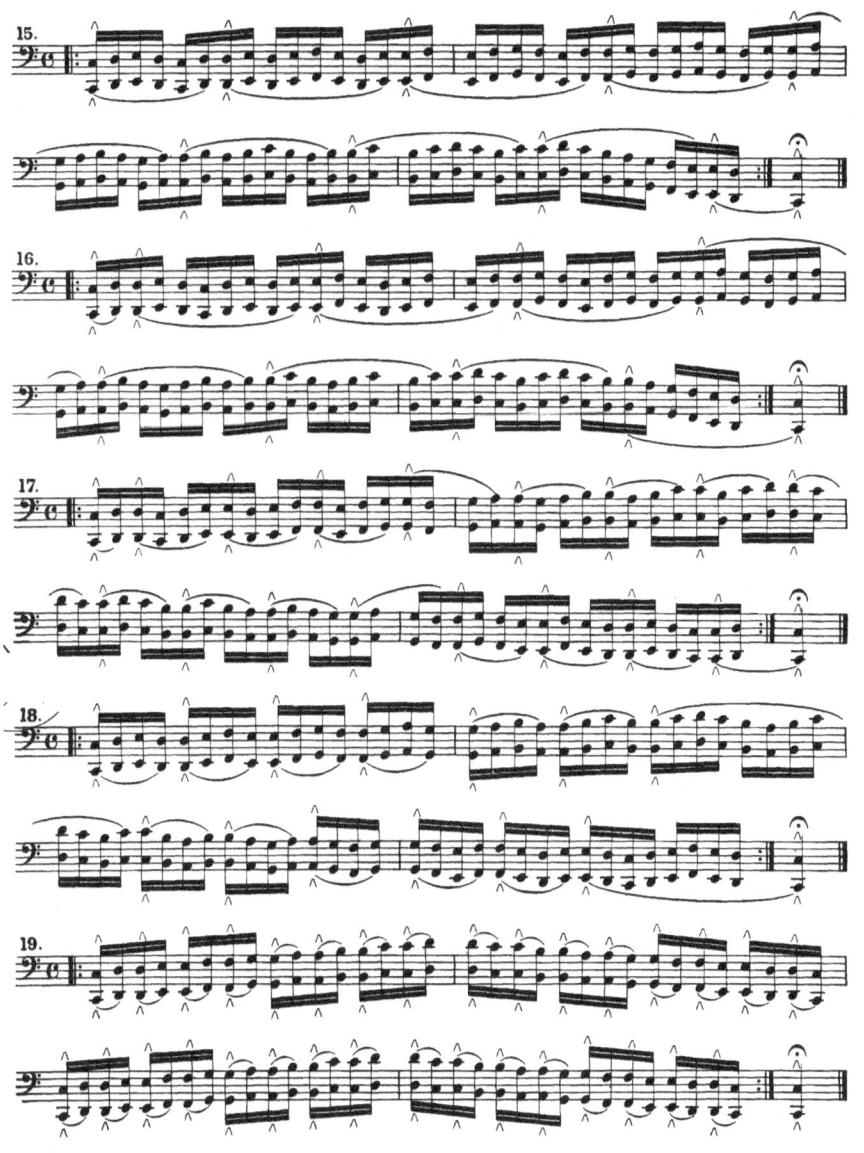

C. Octave Exercises with Skips of a Third.

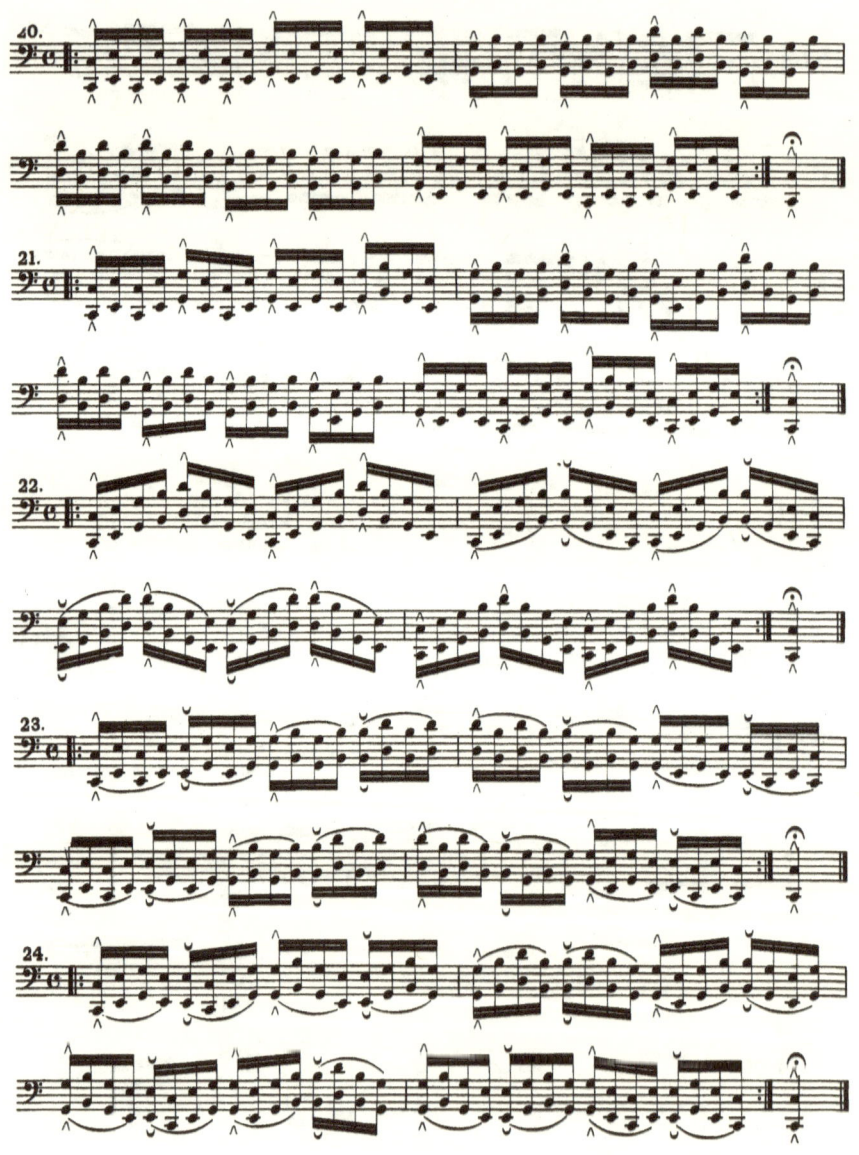

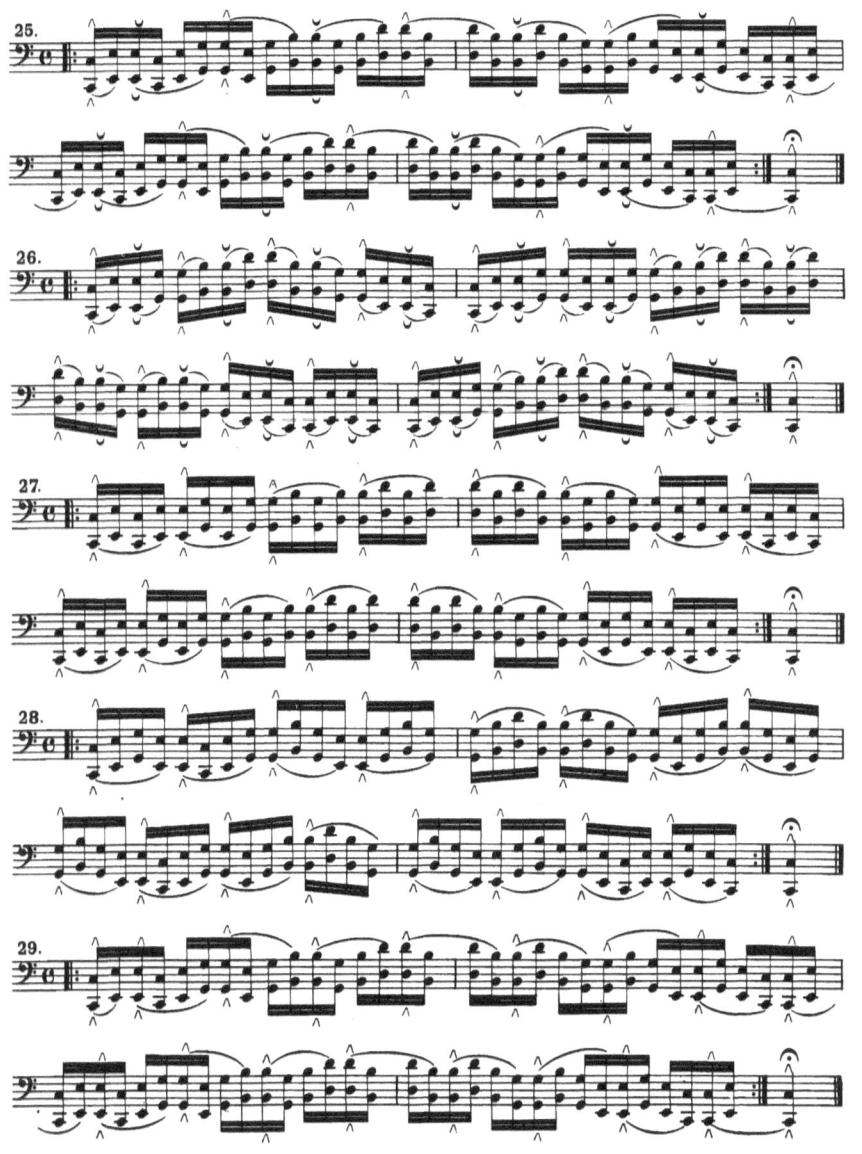

D. Octave Exercises with Mixed Thirds and Seconds.

E. Chromatic Exercises in Octaves.

F. Exercises in Sixths, Solid and Broken.

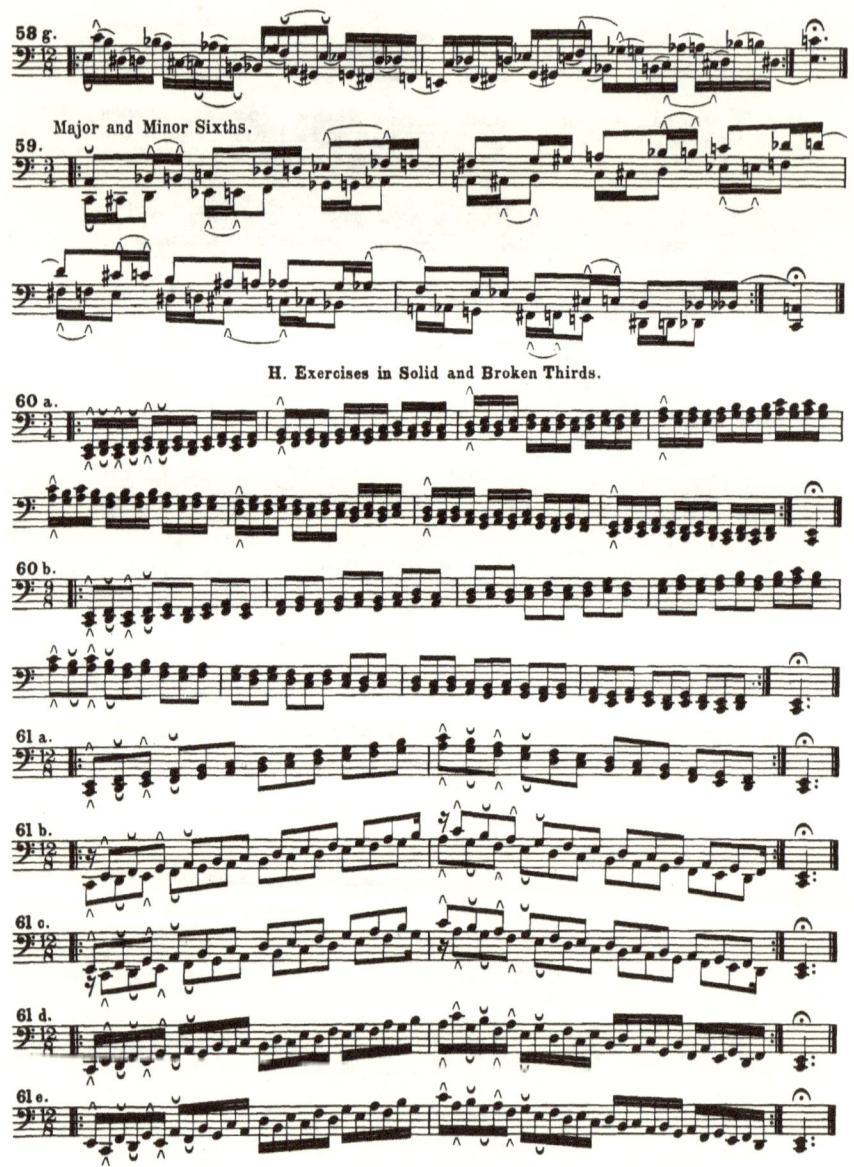

Minor Thirds.

Section III.
A. Exercises on Mixed Intervals.

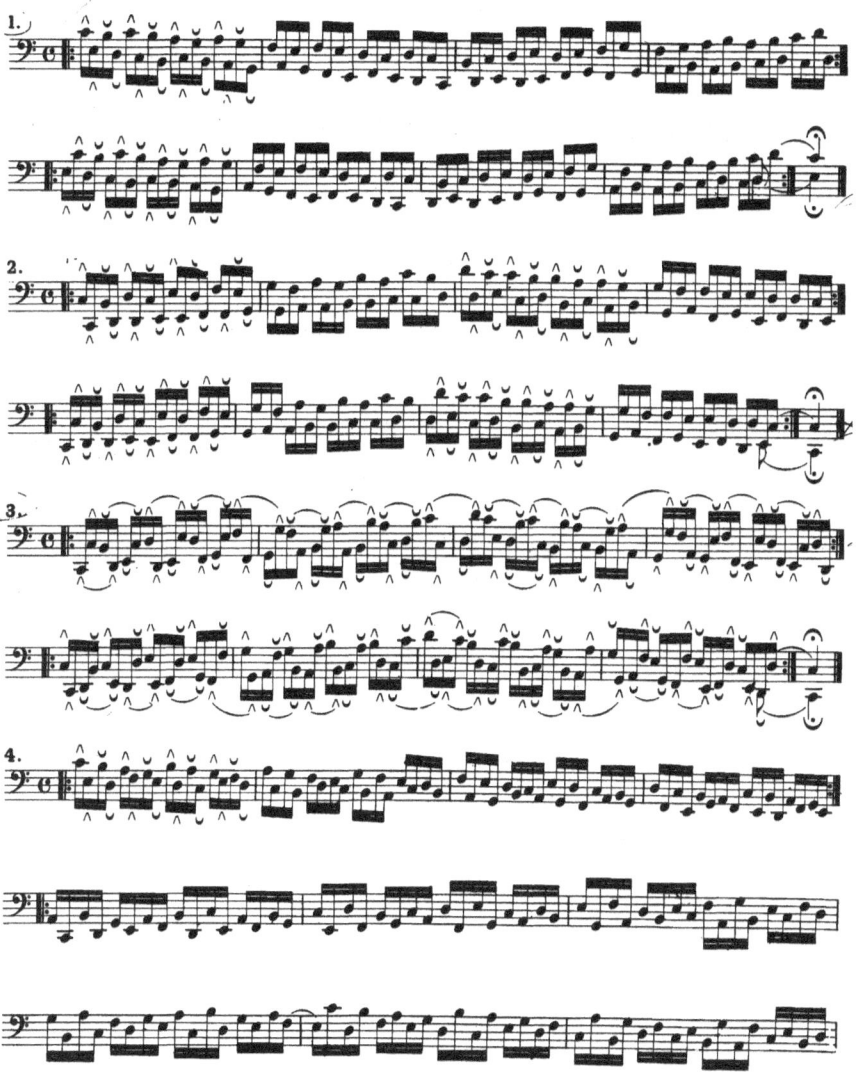

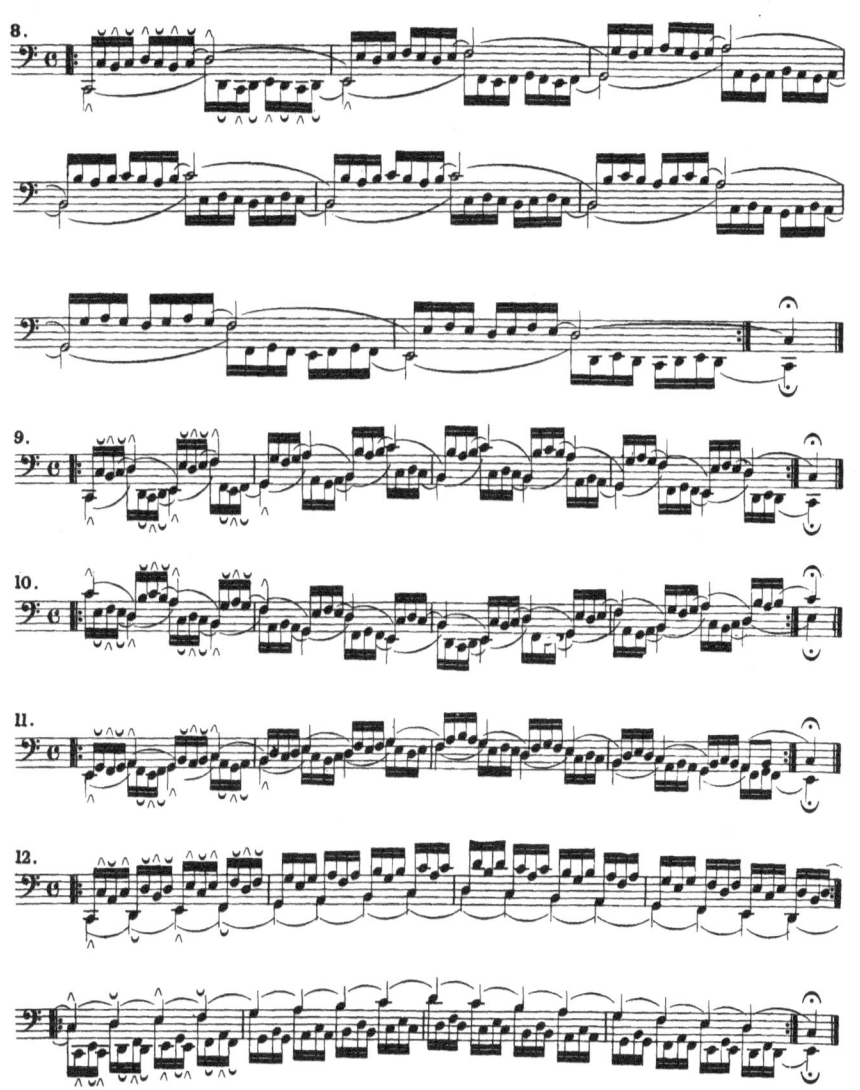

B. Exercises with Mixed Figures.

C. Miscellaneous Exercises.
(For heels alone, or for toes alone.)

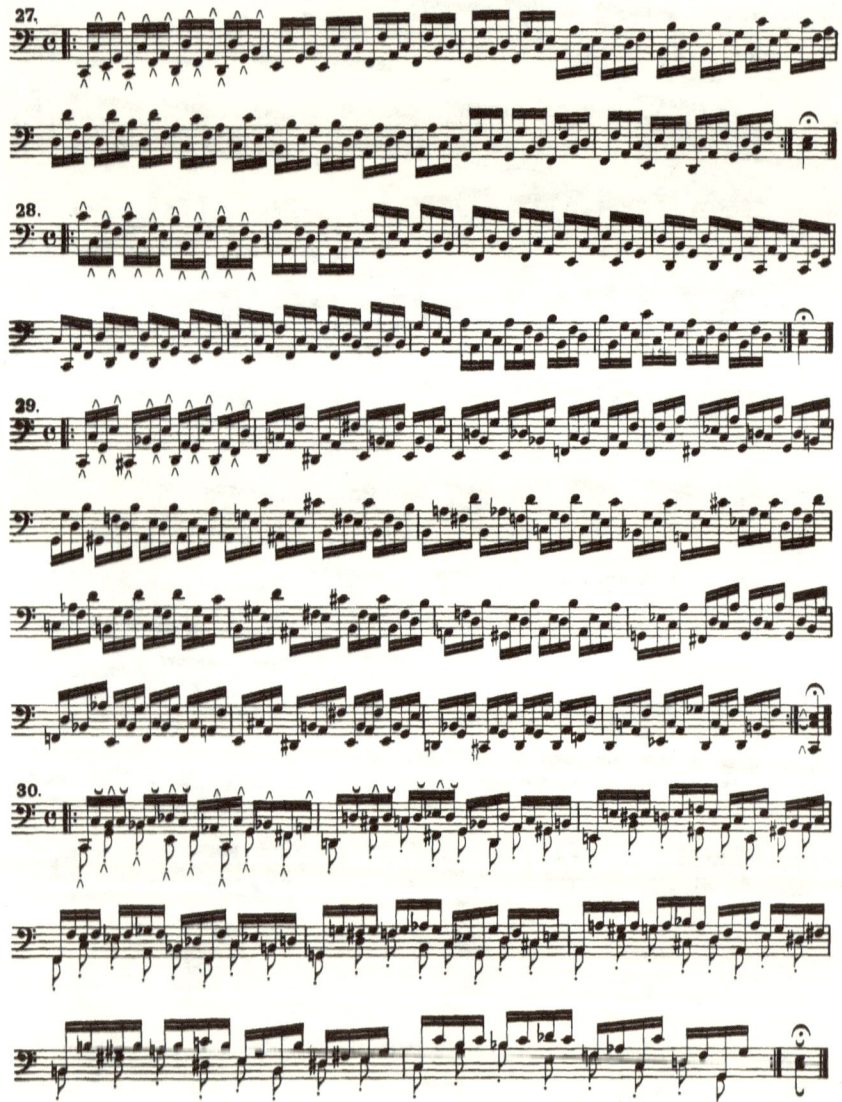

D. Exercises on Changing Feet.

Section IV.
A. Major Scales.

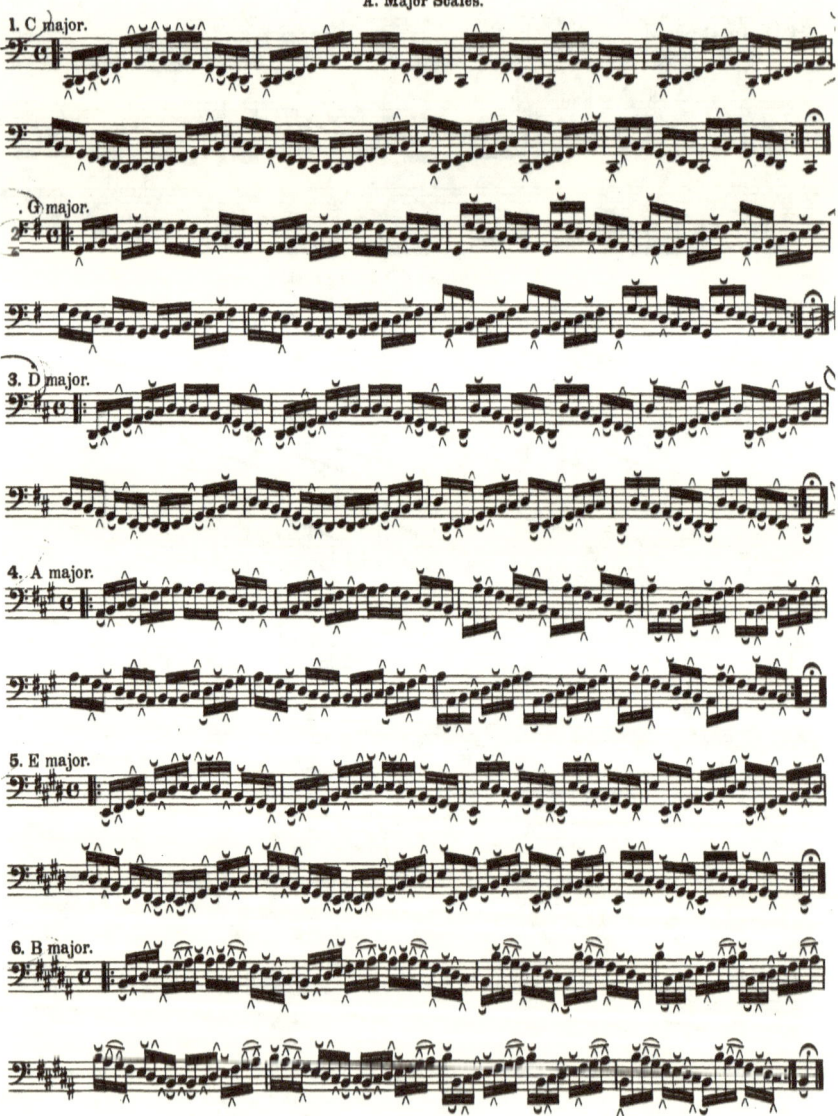

B. Melodic Minor Scales.

13. A minor.

14. E minor.

15. B minor.

16. F sharp minor.

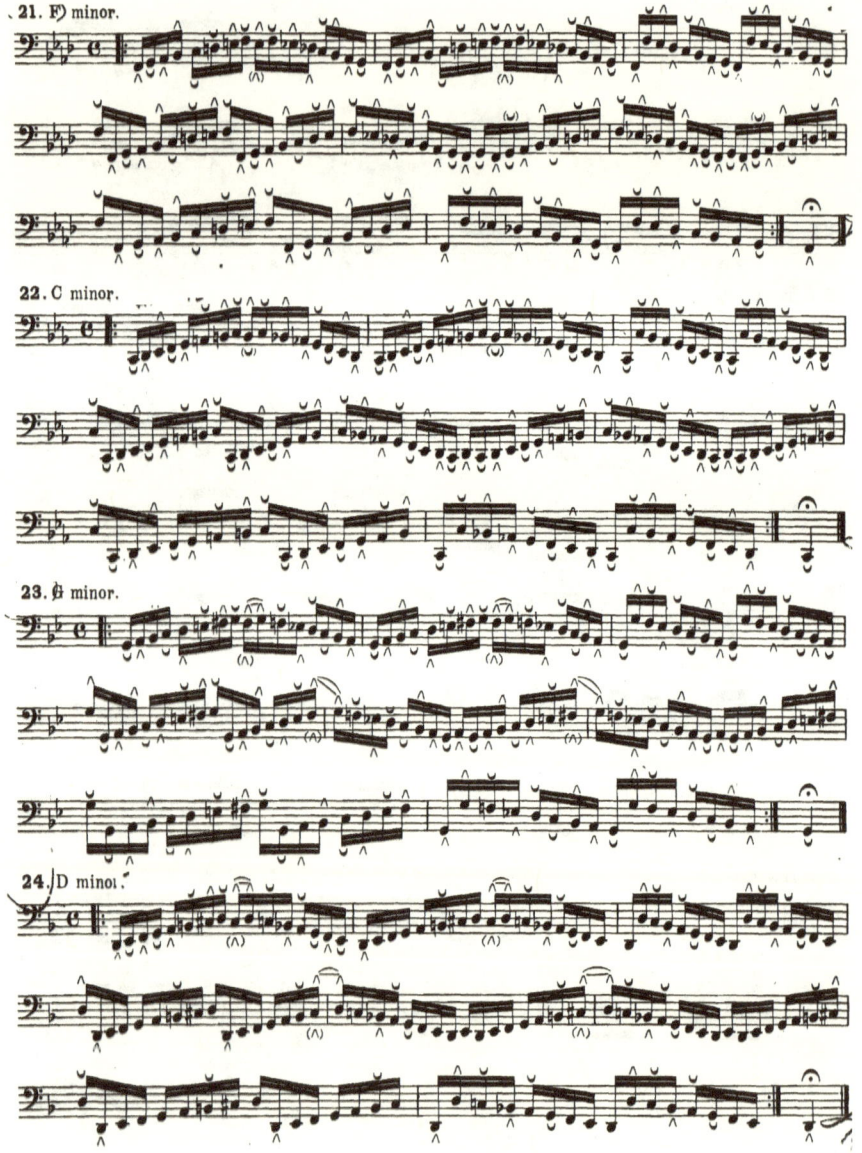

C. Harmonic Minor Scales.*

25. A minor.

26. E minor.

27. B minor.

28. F sharp minor.

* The accidental for the raised seventh is added after the signature, in brackets (♯) or (♮).

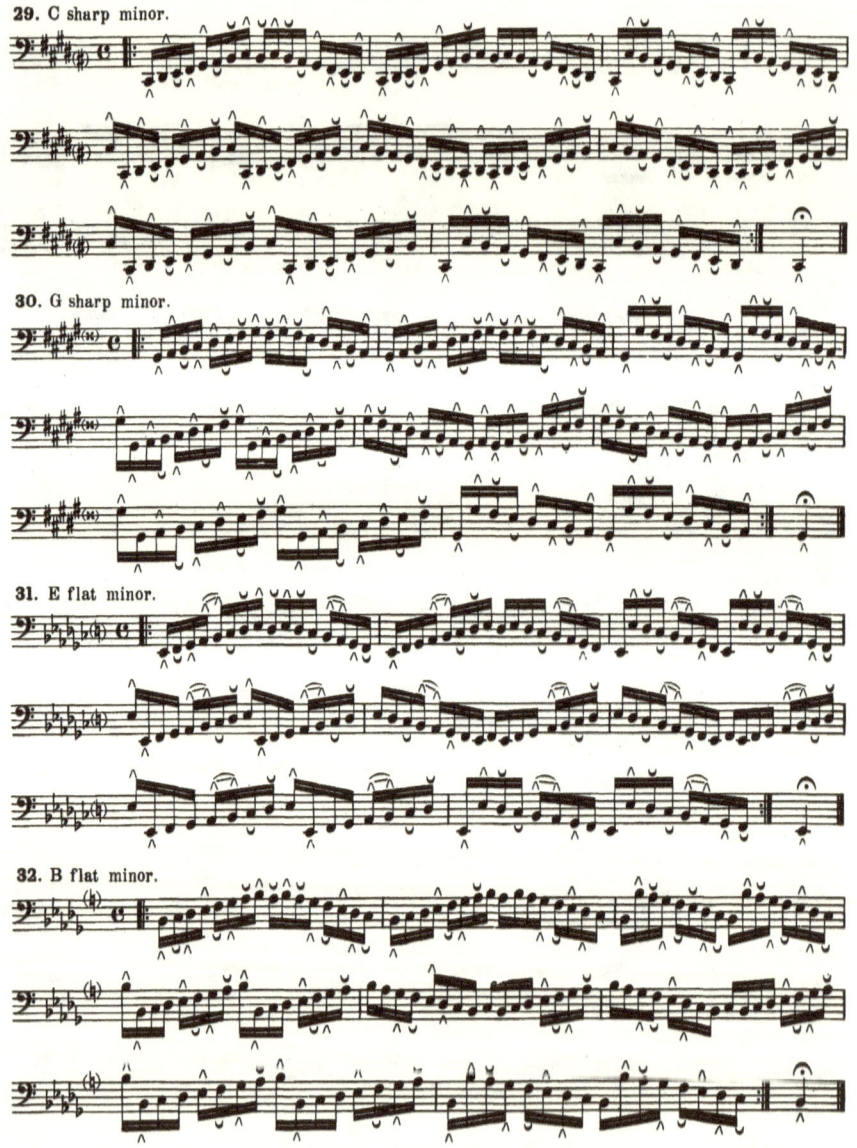

www.ingramcontent.com/pod-product-compliance
Lightning Source LLC
Chambersburg PA
CBHW021800230426
43669CB00006B/142